COOKING WITH
HERBS & SPICES

COOKING WITH HERBS & SPICES

Grange
BOOKS

Published by Grange Books
An imprint of Books & Toys Limited
The Grange
Grange Yard
London SE1 3AG
By arrangement with Ebury Press

ISBN 1 85627 166 8

Consultant editor: Jeni Wright
Editors: Veronica Sperling and Barbara Croxford
Design: Mike Leaman
Illustrations: John Woodcock and Kate Simunek
Photography: David Johnson
Cookery: Susanna Tee, Maxine Clark, Janet Smith

Filmset by Advanced Filmsetters (Glasgow) Ltd

Printed and bound in Italy by
New Interlitho, S.p.a., Milan

CONTENTS

COOKERY NOTES

Follow either metric or imperial measures for the recipes in this book as they are not interchangeable. Sets of spoon measures are available in both metric and imperial size to give accurate measurement of small quantities. All spoon measures are level unless otherwise stated. When measuring milk we have used the exact conversion of 568 ml (1 pint).

* Size 4 eggs should be used except when otherwise stated.

† Granulated sugar is used unless otherwise stated.

● Plain flour is used unless otherwise stated.

OVEN TEMPERATURE CHART

°C	°F	Gas mark
110	225	$\frac{1}{4}$
130	250	$\frac{1}{2}$
140	275	1
150	300	2
170	325	3
180	350	4
190	375	5
200	400	6
220	425	7
230	450	8
240	475	9

KEY TO SYMBOLS

1.00* Indicates minimum preparation and cooking times in hours and minutes. They do not include prepared items in the list of ingredients; calculated times apply only to the method. An asterisk * indicates extra time should be allowed, so check the note below symbols.

⊟ Chef's hats indicate degree of difficulty of a recipe: no hat means it is straightforward; one hat slightly more complicated; two hats indicates that it is for more advanced cooks.

£ Indicates a recipe which is good value for money; £ £ indicates an expensive recipe. No £ sign indicates an inexpensive recipe.

✳ Indicates that a recipe will freeze. If there is no symbol, the recipe is unsuitable for freezing. An asterisk * indicates special freezer instructions so check the note immediately below the symbols.

309 cals Indicates calories per serving, including any suggestions (e.g. cream, to serve) given in the ingredients.

METRIC CONVERSION SCALE

LIQUID			SOLID		
Imperial	Exact conversion	Recommended ml	Imperial	Exact conversion	Recommended g
$\frac{1}{4}$ pint	142 ml	150 ml	1 oz	28.35 g	25 g
$\frac{1}{2}$ pint	284 ml	300 ml	2 oz	56.7 g	50 g
1 pint	568 ml	600 ml	4 oz	113.4 g	100 g
$1\frac{1}{2}$ pints	851 ml	900 ml	8 oz	226.8 g	225 g
$1\frac{3}{4}$ pints	992 ml	1 litre	12 oz	340.2 g	350 g
For quantities of $1\frac{3}{4}$ pints and over, litres and fractions of a litre have been used.			14 oz	397.0 g	400 g
			16 oz (1 lb)	453.6 g	450 g
			1 kilogram (kg) equals 2.2 lb.		

Herbs and Spices

Enter the exotic world of herbs and spices when you open the pages of this book. With recipes from all over the world—some fragrantly fresh with herbs, others sizzlingly spicy—there's something for everyone.

For easy identification of culinary herbs and spices, consult our two-page illustrated "glossary" at the front of the book and familiarise yourself with the different varieties—some familiar, others more unusual but worth getting to know. Then, in the recipe section feast your eyes on dishes for every occasion, from everyday snacks and informal meals to dinner party dishes and cooking for entertaining. There's a chapter each on Soups and Starters, Main Courses—including Meat, Poultry and Game and Fish and Shellfish—Eggs and Cheese, Vegetables, Desserts, and Baking with a photograph of every recipe plus step-by-step illustrations to help you through the method.

At the back of the book you will find a section packed with interesting and useful information: an A–Z of herbs and spices plus a guide in chart form to help you mix and match when cooking; how to make up your own herb and spice mixtures; instructions on growing your own herbs; plus methods of preservation (including a special section on sweet-smelling pot pourri and pomanders—two wonderful ways to make use of a bumper crop). Then in the very last pages of the book, there is a basic recipe collection: how to make your own butters and cheeses, dressings, stuffings and salts, plus oils and vinegars, jellies, mustards, and drinks—all grouped together for easy reference.

CULINARY HERBS AND SPICES

LOVAGE

THYME

MINT

MARJORAM

ROSEMARY

CHERVIL

TARRAGON

PARSLEY

BASIL

BAY

ANGELICA

CURRY PLANT

HORSERADISH
grated

SAGE

DILL, seed, weed

CHIVES

LEMON BALM

OREGANO

GARLIC

LEMON GRASS

CORIANDER,
fresh, ground, seeds

CLOVES

POPPY SEEDS

MUSTARD,
ground, seeds

CARAWAY

SAFFRON

ASAFOETIDA

GINGER

CASSIA

PEPPER

CUMIN,
seeds, ground

CINNAMON,
ground, sticks

JUNIPER

CARDAMOM

STAR ANISE

CHILLI
whole, ground

NUTMEG, whole, ground
MACE

VANILLA PODS

LAOS (galangal)
whole, ground

ALLSPICE

PAPRIKA

FENUGREEK

TURMERIC

CAYENNE

Soups and Starters

Chives, tarragon, paprika, juniper — just some of the delicious herbs and spices used in this chapter to flavour our selection of hot and cold soups, dips, pâtés and tarts which can be served as mouthwatering appetisers to start off a meal on the right note.

ICED SORREL SOUP

| 0.50* | £ ✳* | 177–251 cals |

* plus chilling; freeze after puréeing and before adding cream

Serves 4–6

100 g (4 oz) fresh sorrel

25 g (1 oz) butter or margarine

1 onion, skinned and finely chopped

225 g (8 oz) potatoes, peeled and finely chopped

750 ml (1¼ pints) chicken stock

salt and freshly ground pepper

142 ml (5 fl oz) soured cream

croûtons and single cream, to garnish

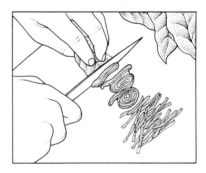

1 Wash the sorrel leaves thoroughly under cold running water and roughly shred the leaves. Then melt the butter or margarine in a pan and fry the onion for 5 minutes until soft.

2 Add the sorrel and cook gently for a further 2–3 minutes until soft. Add the potatoes, stock and seasonings. Bring to the boil, then cover and simmer for 20 minutes.

3 Cool slightly then push through a sieve or purée in an electric blender or food processor. Stir in the soured cream and chill well. Serve garnished with croûtons and cream.

Menu Suggestion
Serve with Minted Lamb Grill (page 27) and Chocolate and Vanilla Roulade (page 113).

11

DEEP-FRIED MUSHROOMS WITH HERBY DRESSING

0.30* | f | 318 cals

* plus 30 minutes cooling and 2 hours chilling

Serves 4

75 ml (5 tbsp) thick homemade
   mayonnaise (see page 151)

75 ml (5 tbsp) soured cream

30 ml (2 tbsp) chopped capers

15 ml (1 tbsp) tarragon vinegar

15 ml (1 tbsp) chopped fresh
   tarragon or 7.5 ml (1½ tsp) dried

15 ml (1 tbsp) snipped fresh chives

salt and freshly ground pepper

50 g (2 oz) plain flour plus a little
   extra, for coating

30 ml (2 tbsp) maize flour

30 ml (2 tbsp) arrowroot

300 ml (½ pint) iced water

450 g (1 lb) button mushrooms,
   wiped and trimmed

vegetable oil, for deep-frying

tarragon or parsley sprigs, to
   garnish

1 Make the herby dressing. Put mayonnaise, soured cream, capers, vinegar, tarragon, chives and seasoning in a bowl and whisk well. Turn into a bowl, cover and refrigerate for at least 2 hours.

2 Make the mushroom batter. Sift flours and arrowroot into bowl; gradually whisk in water. Cover, refrigerate for 30 minutes.

3 Coat the mushrooms lightly in flour; dip into batter. Heat oil in a wok or deep-fat frier, then drop in mushrooms a few at a time.

4 Fry for 1–2 minutes until they rise to the surface of the oil and are golden brown.

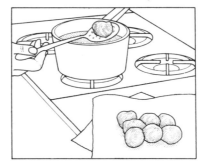

5 Remove the mushrooms from the oil with a slotted spoon and drain on absorbent kitchen paper. Keep hot in the oven while frying the remainder.

6 Pile the mushrooms on four individual serving plates and garnish with tarragon or parsley sprigs. Serve at once, with the dressing handed separately.

Menu Suggestion
Serve with Gingered Japanese Chicken (page 62) and Geranium Grape Sorbet (page 115).

SPICY CRAB DIP

| 0.15* | £ £ | 136 cals |

*plus 2 hours chilling

Serves 4

225 g (8 oz) cottage cheese

225 g (8 oz) frozen white crabmeat, thawed

45 ml (3 tbsp) finely chopped canned pimiento

10 ml (2 tsp) Worcestershire sauce

5 ml (1 tsp) anchovy essence

2.5 ml ($\frac{1}{2}$ tsp) cayenne pepper

juice of $\frac{1}{2}$ lemon

salt and freshly ground pepper

sticks of raw celery, carrot and cucumber, cauliflower florets, spring onions and small whole radishes, to serve

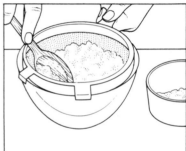

1 Work the cottage cheese through a sieve into a bowl. Flake the crabmeat, then fold into the sieved cottage cheese until evenly mixed.

2 Fold in the pimiento, then stir in the Worcestershire sauce, anchovy essence, half the cayenne, the lemon juice and salt and ground pepper to taste.

3 Turn the dip into a serving bowl, then sprinkle with the remaining cayenne. Chill in the refrigerator for at least 2 hours until serving time. Serve the dip chilled, with a platter of raw vegetables.

Menu Suggestion
Serve with Afelia (page 30) and Lemon Balm Syllabub (page 105).

GOULASH SOUP WITH CARAWAY DUMPLINGS

| 2.45 | 🍴 | £ | ✳* | 515–772 cals |

* freeze without dumplings

Serves 4–6

700 g (1½ lb) silverside or lean chuck steak

salt and freshly ground pepper

25 g (1 oz) butter

2 onions, skinned and chopped

1 small green pepper, seeded and chopped

4 tomatoes, skinned and quartered

141-g (5-oz) can tomato paste

600 ml (1 pint) rich beef stock

15 ml (1 tbsp) paprika

450 g (1 lb) potatoes, peeled

100 g (4 oz) self-raising flour

50 g (2 oz) shredded suet

5 ml (1 tsp) caraway seeds

chopped fresh parsley, to garnish

142 ml (5 fl oz) soured cream

1 Remove any excess fat or gristle from the silverside or chuck steak and cut the meat into small pieces. Season well.

2 Melt the butter in a large saucepan, add the onions and green pepper and sauté for 10 minutes until tender.

3 Add the meat pieces, tomatoes, tomato paste, stock and paprika. Stir well and bring to the boil. Reduce the heat, cover and simmer for 2½ hours, stirring occasionally.

4 Half an hour before the end of cooking, cut the potatoes into bite-sized pieces, bring to the boil in salted water and simmer until cooked. Drain well and add to the soup while it is simmering.

5 Make the dumplings. Put the flour, suet, caraway seeds and seasoning in a bowl and add enough cold water to form a firm mixture. Roll into about sixteen small dumplings.

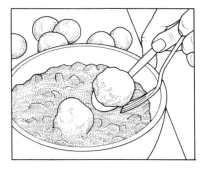

6 Twenty minutes before end of cooking, drop dumplings into the soup, cover and simmer until the dumplings are cooked.

7 Garnish with chopped parsley and serve the soured cream separately, for each person to spoon into their soup.

Menu Suggestion
Serve with fresh French bread and butter and a tossed green salad.

GOULASH

Goulash soup is simply a more liquid version of goulash, with a similar base of meat and potatoes for easy eating. Both are popular in Austria and Hungary —no-one is quite sure in which country the recipe first originated.

Austrian goulash is usually a simple dish made with beef and potatoes, while Hungarian goulash is often made with veal and far more ingredients— usually red and green peppers and mushrooms, sometimes sauerkraut and smoked pork sausage as well. Four ingredients which are common to all goulash recipes are caraway seeds, onions, paprika and tomatoes —the latter giving the dish its characteristic bright red colour. Dumplings and soured cream are optional extras.

LEEKS À LA VINAIGRETTE

0.30*	£	467–600 cals

* plus 30 minutes chilling

Serves 4–6

12 small leeks
salt and freshly ground pepper
150 ml ($\frac{1}{4}$ pint) olive oil
60 ml (4 tbsp) red wine vinegar
15 ml (1 tbsp) tomato purée
15 ml (1 tbsp) coriander seeds,
  lightly crushed
2.5 ml ($\frac{1}{2}$ tsp) sugar
coriander sprigs, to garnish
hot garlic bread, to serve

1 Trim the root ends of the leeks and cut off the damaged tops. Then slit each leek lengthways in two or three places.

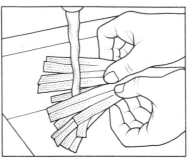

2 Hold under cold running water and wash away any grit caught between the leaves. Cook the leeks in boiling salted water for 6–8 minutes until just tender. Drain, refresh under cold running water, then leave to drain and dry on absorbent kitchen paper.

3 Make the dressing. Put the oil and vinegar in a bowl with the tomato purée, coriander seeds, sugar and salt and pepper to taste. Whisk vigorously with a fork until thick.

4 Arrange the cold leeks in a shallow serving dish and pour the dressing over them. Chill in the refrigerator for at least 30 minutes before serving. Garnish with sprigs of coriander and serve with hot garlic bread.

Menu Suggestion
Serve with Rabbit Casserole with Sage Dumplings (page 55) and Rhubarb and Orange Fool (page 111).

STUFFED COURGETTES WITH WALNUTS AND SAGE

| 1.20 | 🗋 | £ | 422 cals |

Serves 4

4 large courgettes, total weight about 700 g (1½ lb)

1 onion, skinned and chopped

90 g (3½ oz) butter or margarine

50 g (2 oz) walnut pieces, chopped

50 g (2 oz) fresh white breadcrumbs

10 ml (2 tsp) chopped fresh sage

15 ml (1 tbsp) tomato purée

1 egg, beaten

salt and freshly ground pepper

30 ml (2 tbsp) plain flour

300 ml (½ pint) chicken stock

30 ml (2 tbsp) chopped parsley

walnut halves and fresh sage sprigs, to garnish

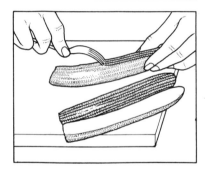

1 Wipe the courgettes. Using a fork, score down skin at 1-cm (½-inch) intervals, then halve each one lengthwise.

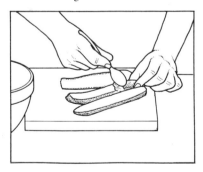

2 Hollow out the centres of the courgettes using a teaspoon. Blanch in boiling water for 4 minutes, drain, then hold under cold tap. Cool for 15–20 minutes.

3 Make the stuffing. Fry the onion in 25 g (1 oz) butter for 5–10 minutes until golden. Remove from heat and stir in half the walnuts, breadcrumbs, half the sage, the tomato purée, beaten egg and plenty of seasoning. Sandwich the courgettes with the stuffing.

4 Place in a buttered ovenproof dish and dot with a little more butter. Cover the courgettes and bake in the oven at 190°C (375°F) mark 5 for about 30 minutes.

5 Meanwhile, make the sauce. Melt 50 g (2 oz) butter in a pan, stir in the flour and cook gently for 1 minute, stirring.

6 Remove from the heat and gradually stir in the stock. Bring to the boil and continue to cook, stirring until the sauce thickens. Stir in the parsley, seasoning and remaining sage and walnuts. Remove from heat and cover the sauce.

7 To serve, reheat the sauce. Pour some over the courgettes and serve the rest separately. Garnish with walnut halves and sage sprigs.

Menu Suggestion

Serve with Porc au Poivre (page 35) and Summer Fruit Salad (page 106).

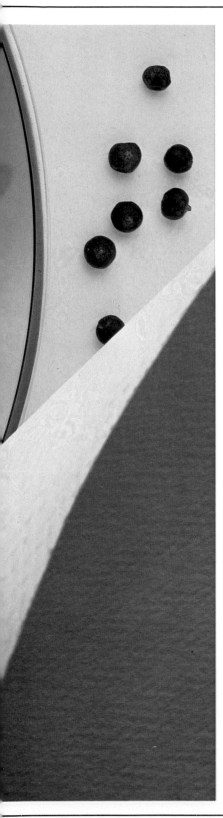

PORK PÂTÉ WITH SAGE AND JUNIPER BERRIES

| 2.15* | f | 245 cals |

* plus prepare a day ahead; 1 hour soaking and overnight chilling

Serves 12

175 g (6 oz) pig's liver, washed and sliced

45 ml (3 tbsp) milk

175 g (6 oz) streaky bacon rashers, rinded

50 g (2 oz) shallots, skinned and chopped

225 g (8 oz) pork belly

225 g (8 oz) pork sausagemeat

5 ml (1 tsp) sea salt

2.5 ml ($\frac{1}{2}$ tsp) black peppercorns

10 juniper berries

2 garlic cloves, skinned

15 ml (1 tbsp) chopped fresh sage or 5 ml (1 tsp) dried

1 egg, beaten

25 g (1 oz) fresh white breadcrumbs

30 ml (2 tbsp) single cream

fresh sage sprigs, to garnish

1 The day before, soak the liver in the milk for about an hour to remove its bitter flavour. Remove and pat dry with absorbent kitchen paper.

2 Using the back of a knife, stretch 100 g (4 oz) of the bacon rashers and use to line a 450-g (1-lb) loaf tin.

3 Using an electric mincer or a food processor, mince the liver, chopped shallots, remaining bacon and pork belly. Combine with the sausagemeat.

4 Crush the sea salt, peppercorns, juniper berries and garlic cloves in a mortar. Add to the pork mixture with the sage, egg, breadcrumbs and cream and mix well together.

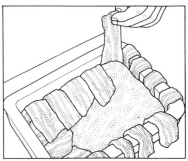

5 Press the mixture into the bacon-lined dish. Fold the rasher ends over the mixture and cover the dish tightly.

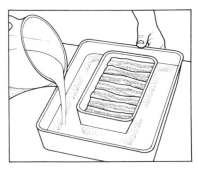

6 Half fill a roasting tin with boiling water and place loaf tin in it. Cook in the oven at 170°C (325°F) mark 3 for 1$\frac{3}{4}$ hours.

7 Remove from water bath, leave to cool then weight down. Refrigerate overnight. Allow to stand at room temperature for 30 minutes. Serve sliced, garnished with sage sprigs.

Menu Suggestion
Serve with fresh French bread and butter or Hot Potatoes with Dill (page 93) and a mixed or green salad.

STUFFED TARRAGON TOMATOES

| 0.30* | £ | 365 cals |

* plus 30 minutes chilling

Serves 4

4 large firm tomatoes

salt

100 g (4 oz) full fat soft cheese

30 ml (2 tbsp) thick homemade mayonnaise (see page 151)

1 bunch of spring onions, trimmed and very finely chopped

30 ml (2 tbsp) chopped fresh tarragon

freshly ground pepper

90 ml (6 tbsp) sunflower or corn oil

30 ml (2 tbsp) tarragon wine vinegar

1.25 ml ($\frac{1}{4}$ tsp) mustard powder

pinch of sugar

tarragon sprigs, to garnish

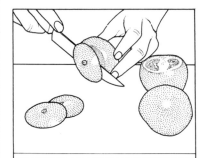

1 Cut a slice off the top of each tomato and set aside.

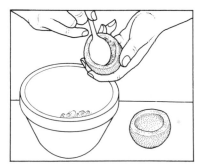

2 Using a sharp-edged teaspoon, carefully scoop out the pulp and seeds from the insides of the tomatoes. Then sprinkle the insides lightly with salt and stand upside down to drain.

3 Meanwhile, mix the cheese with the mayonnaise, spring onions, half the tarragon and salt and pepper to taste. Spoon the cheese mixture into the tomato cases and replace the reserved slices at an angle.

4 Put the oil and vinegar in a bowl with the remaining tarragon, the mustard, sugar and salt and pepper to taste. Whisk with a fork until thick, then pour slowly over the tomatoes. Chill in the refrigerator for 30 minutes, then garnish with tarragon sprigs and serve on individual plates.

Menu Suggestion

Serve with Lamb with Rosemary and Garlic (page 28) and Poached Pears in Ginger Syrup (page 114).

PRAWN AND DILL TARTLETS

| 1.00 | 🗂 £ £ ✳ | 462 cals |

Makes 6

75 g (3 oz) butter

25 g (1 oz) blended white vegetable fat

175 g (6 oz) plain flour

45 ml (3 tbsp) water

50 g (2 oz) spring onions, washed and finely chopped

2 egg yolks

200 ml (7 fl oz) double cream

2.5 ml ($\frac{1}{2}$ tsp) chopped fresh dill or 1.25 ml ($\frac{1}{4}$ tsp) dried

salt and freshly ground pepper

36 fresh prawns, peeled

6 unshelled prawns, to garnish

1 Make the pastry. Rub the fats into the flour and bind to a firm dough with the water. Knead lightly until just smooth. Chill in the refrigerator for 15 minutes.

2 Roll out the pastry thinly and use to line six individual fluted flan dishes. Bake the pastry 'blind' for 15 minutes until just set and beginning to colour.

3 Divide onions between flan dishes. Make custard mixture. Mix egg yolks, cream, dill and seasoning together and pour into the cases to fill two-thirds deep.

4 Arrange the prawns in the custard mixture, and bake in the oven at 170°C (325°F) mark 3 for 20 minutes until set. Garnish and serve warm, not hot.

Menu Suggestion
Serve with Duck with Spiced Stuffing (page 47) and Poached Pears in Ginger Syrup (page 114).

MUSSELS WITH GARLIC AND PARSLEY

1.00*	439–593 cals

* plus 20 minutes soaking

Serves 4–6

2.3 litres (4 pints) or 1.1–1.4 kg (2½–3 lb) mussels in their shells

150 ml (10 tbsp) fresh breadcrumbs

150 ml (10 tbsp) chopped fresh parsley

2 garlic cloves, skinned and finely chopped

freshly ground black pepper

100 ml (4 fl oz) olive oil

30 ml (2 tbsp) grated Parmesan cheese

lemon wedges and French bread, to serve

1 To clean the mussels, put them in a sink and scrub them thoroughly with a hard brush in several changes of water.

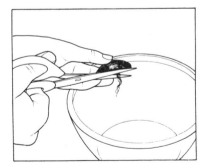

2 Scrape off any barnacles with a sharp knife. Then, with a pair of scissors, cut off any beards, or tufts of hair which may protrude from the shell.

3 Leave mussels to soak in a bowl of cold water for 20 minutes, then discard any that are not tightly closed or do not close on giving them a sharp tap.

4 Drain the mussels and place in a large saucepan. Cover and cook over high heat for 5–10 minutes until the mussels are open, shaking the pan frequently. Shell the mussels, reserving one half of each empty shell.

5 Strain the mussel liquid through a sieve lined with absorbent kitchen paper. Mix together the breadcrumbs, parsley, garlic and plenty of pepper. Add the oil and 60 ml (4 tbsp) of the mussel liquid. Blend well together. Taste and adjust the seasonings.

6 Place the mussels in their shells on two baking sheets. With your fingers, pick up a good pinch of the breadcrumb mixture and press it down on each mussel, covering it well and filling the shell. Sprinkle with the Parmesan.

7 Bake in the oven at 230°C (450°F) mark 8 for 10 minutes, swapping the baking sheets over halfway through the cooking time. Serve with French bread.

Menu Suggestion

Serve with Sorrel Stuffed Lamb (page 35) and Summer Fruit Salad (page 106).

MUSSELS

Mussels are an inexpensive starter, yet nonetheless everyone thinks of them as something very special. Some people are nervous of eating mussels however, because they are unsure whether they have come from polluted waters or not. This nervousness is completely unnecessary nowadays because all mussels offered for sale must undergo a special cleaning process. As long as you buy them fresh on the day you intend to eat them, from a reputable fishmonger, there is absolutely no cause for concern.

When buying mussels allow for wastage—buy at least 350 g (12 oz) or 450 ml (¾ pint) per person to be sure of having enough for a starter.

Follow these few guidelines to help you to prepare mussels.
- Scrub the shells very thoroughly with a stiff vegetable brush to remove all traces of dirt and sand. Scrubbing under cold running water is the most efficient way to do this.
- Scrape off barnacles with a sharp knife and remove the "beard" which protrudes between the two shells.
- Discard any that are open or which don't close when given a sharp tap against a work surface. This may seem rather wasteful but it is a very important part of the preparation process—any mussel that remains open cannot be alive and should not be cooked.
- Steam or cook the drained mussels according to individual recipes, allowing 5–10 minutes cooking time over high heat. Always cover the pan and shake frequently during cooking. Don't cook for longer than this or the mussel 'meat' will toughen and become coarse and rubbery.
- At the end of cooking, discard any mussels that haven't opened.

SHAMEE KEBAB WITH YOGURT MINT DIP

1.35* ☐ £ ✳* 381 cals

* plus 2 hours cooling and chilling;
freeze after stage 5

Serves 6

100 g (4 oz) brown, green or red
    lentils

450 g (1 lb) minced raw lamb or
    beef

2 onions, skinned and chopped

2 garlic cloves, skinned and
    crushed with 5 ml (1 tsp) salt

15 ml (1 tbsp) ground coriander

15 ml (1 tbsp) ground cumin

10 ml (2 tsp) ground ginger

1.25 ml ($\frac{1}{4}$ tsp) chilli powder, or to
    taste

142 g (5 oz) natural yogurt

60 ml (4 tbsp) chopped fresh mint

10 ml (2 tsp) sugar

2.5 ml ($\frac{1}{2}$ tsp) cayenne pepper

salt

50 g (2 oz) unsalted butter, softened

freshly ground pepper

about 60 ml (4 tbsp) ghee (see page
    148) or vegetable oil

5 ml (1 tsp) ground turmeric

few drops of red food colouring

lettuce leaves or fresh coriander
    and lemon wedges, to garnish

1 Rinse the lentils under cold
running water. Put in a large,
heavy-based saucepan with the
meat, half the onion, the garlic and
spices. Pour in just enough water
to cover and bring to boil, stirring.

2 Lower the heat and simmer
for 45 minutes to 1 hour until
all the water is absorbed and the
mixture is thick. Stir frequently
during this time. Tip into a bowl
and leave to cool for 1–2 hours.

3 Meanwhile, make the dip. Put
the yogurt, remaining onion,
mint, sugar, cayenne pepper and
2.5 ml ($\frac{1}{2}$ tsp) salt in a blender or
food processor and work until
evenly combined. Turn into a
bowl and chill for at least 2 hours.

4 Work the lentil and meat mixture to a smooth paste in
batches in a food processor or an
electric blender, adding a little of
the butter with each batch. Add
salt and pepper to taste.

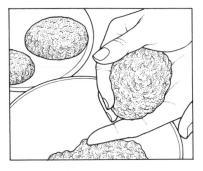

5 Shape the mixture into twenty-
four oval shapes with your
hands. Chill in the refrigerator for
at least 30 minutes.

6 Heat half the ghee or oil in a
frying-pan, then stir in the
turmeric and food colouring. Add
the kebabs a few at a time and fry
over moderate heat for a few minutes on each side until crisp and
nicely coloured.

7 Remove from the pan with a
slotted spoon and keep hot in
the oven while frying the remainder, adding more ghee or oil
when necessary.

8 Serve the kebabs hot, garnished with lettuce or coriander
and wedges of lemon. Hand the
dip separately.

Menu Suggestion
Serve with Seafood Curry
(page 76) and Sag Aloo (page 97).

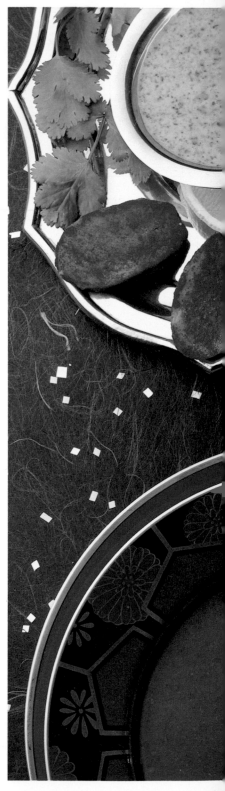

MULLIGATAWNY SOUP

| 1.15 | £ | ✳* | 204 cals |

* freeze after stage 3

Serves 6

50 g (2 oz) butter

1 onion, skinned and finely
   chopped

100 g (4 oz) carrot, peeled and finely
   chopped

100 g (4 oz) swede, peeled and finely
   chopped

1 small eating apple, peeled and
   finely chopped

50 g (2 oz) streaky bacon, rinded
   and finely chopped

25 g (1 oz) plain flour

15 ml (1 tbsp) mild curry paste

15 ml (1 tbsp) tomato purée

30 ml (2 tbsp) mango chutney

1.4 litres (2½ pints) beef stock

5 ml (1 tsp) dried mixed herbs

pinch of ground mace

pinch of ground cloves

salt and freshly ground pepper

50 g (2 oz) long grain rice

coriander sprigs, to garnish

1 Melt the butter in a large
   saucepan and fry the onion,
carrot, swede, apple and bacon
until lightly browned.

2 Stir in the flour, curry paste,
   tomato purée and chutney.
Cook for 1–2 minutes, then add
remaining ingredients, except rice.

3 Bring to the boil, skim and
   simmer, covered, for 30–40
minutes. Sieve the soup or purée
in a blender or food processor.

4 Return the soup to the pan,
   bring to the boil, add the rice
and boil gently for about 12 minutes, until the rice is tender. Pour
into a bowl and garnish.

Menu Suggestion
Serve with Turkey in Spiced
Yogurt (page 52) and Sweet Indian
Saffron Rice (page 108).

MAIN COURSES

Meat

British, French, Greek, German, Indian, Indonesian and even South African recipes — in this chapter you'll find a vast choice of different ideas from different countries, for everyday suppers and dinners and for entertaining. Herby and spicy marinades feature in many of the recipes, for the simple reason that there is no better way to ensure that meat is tender, succulent and full of flavour.

MINTED LAMB GRILL

0.25* ✳* 255 cals

* plus 1 hour marinating; freeze in the marinade

Serves 4

4 lamb chump chops
30 ml (2 tbsp) chopped fresh mint or 15 ml (1 tbsp) dried
20 ml (4 tsp) white wine vinegar
30 ml (2 tbsp) clear honey
salt and freshly ground pepper
fresh mint sprigs, to garnish

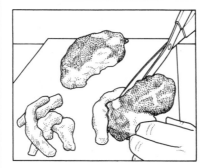

1 Trim any excess fat off the chump chops using a pair of sharp kitchen scissors.

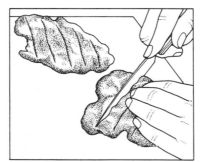

2 With a knife, slash both sides of the chops to a depth of about 5 mm ($\frac{1}{4}$ inch).

3 Make the marinade. Mix the chopped fresh mint, vinegar, honey and seasonings together, stirring well.

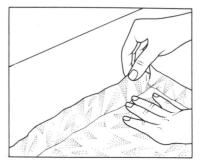

4 Place a sheet of foil in the grill pan and turn up the edges to prevent marinade running into pan.

5 Place the chops side by side on the foil and spoon over the marinade. Leave in a cool place for about 1 hour, basting occasionally.

6 Grill under a moderate heat for 5–6 minutes on each side, turning once only. Baste with the marinade during the cooking time. Garnish with mint before serving.

Menu Suggestion
Serve with Pork Pâté with Sage and Juniper Berries (page 19) and Chocolate and Vanilla Roulade (page 113).

MINT
This herb has a natural affinity with lamb, but did you know there are many different kinds? *Spearmint* is perhaps the best known, and is a well-known cure for indigestion as well as being used as a culinary herb. *Apple-mint* is woolly in appearance compared with spearmint, and has the flavour of apples and spearmint combined together. It goes particularly well with lamb, and is excellent for making mint sauce and mint jelly. *Peppermint* is yet another kind of mint; it has a strong scent and flavour — its oil is used in the making of sweets — and is also sometimes called brandy mint.

LAMB WITH ROSEMARY AND GARLIC

| 3.15* | £ | ✳* | 305 cals |

* plus 12 hours standing; freeze after
stage 3

Serves 6

2-kg (4¼-lb) leg of lamb
2 large garlic cloves, skinned
50 g (2 oz) butter, softened
**15 ml (1 tbsp) chopped fresh
    rosemary or 5 ml (1 tsp) dried**
salt and freshly ground pepper
30 ml (2 tbsp) plain flour
450 ml (¾ pint) chicken stock
fresh rosemary sprigs, to garnish

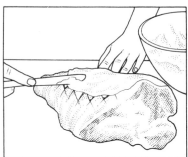

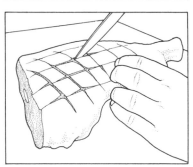

1 Using a sharp knife, score the
surface of the lamb into a
diamond pattern to the depth of
about 12 mm (½ inch).

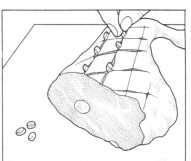

2 Cut the cloves of garlic into
wafer thin slices. Push the
slices into the scored surface of the
lamb with your fingers.

3 Mix the butter with the rosemary and seasoning and then
spread all over the lamb. Place the
joint in a shallow dish, cover tightly
with cling film and refrigerate for
at least 12 hours.

4 Uncover the lamb and transfer
it to a medium roasting tin.
Place in the oven and cook at
180°C (350°F) mark 4 for about
2¼ hours, basting occasionally as
the fat begins to run. Pierce the
joint with a fine skewer; when done
the juices should run clear at first,
then with a hint of red.

5 Place the joint on a serving
plate, cover loosely and keep
warm in a low oven. Pour all excess fat out of the roasting tin
leaving about 45 ml (3 tbsp) fat
with the meat juices. Sprinkle the
flour into the roasting tin and stir
until evenly mixed. Cook over a
gentle heat for 2–3 minutes until
well browned, stirring frequently.

6 Add the stock and seasoning
and bring to the boil, stirring.
Simmer for 3–4 minutes, adjust
the seasoning. To serve, garnish
the lamb with rosemary and serve
the gravy separately.

Menu Suggestion
Serve with Prawn and Dill
Tartlets (page 21), Peppered
Carrots (page 98) and Rhubarb
and Orange Fool (page 111).

AFELIA
(GREEK PORK AND CORIANDER CASSEROLE)

| 1.15* | £ | ✳* | 380–570 cals |

* plus overnight marinating; freeze
before garnishing in stage 2

Serves 4–6

700–900 g (1½–2 lb) boneless pork
  shoulder, cut into bite-sized
  pieces

150 ml (¼ pint) full-bodied red wine

30 ml (2 tbsp) crushed coriander
  seeds

60 ml (4 tbsp) olive oil

salt and freshly ground pepper

fresh coriander sprigs, to garnish

1 Put the pork in an earthenware
  dish, pour over the wine and
sprinkle with the coriander. Stir
well; cover and leave to marinate
in a cool place overnight.

2 Next day, remove pork from
  the marinade using a slotted
spoon. Reserve marinade. Heat oil
in a flameproof casserole, add pork
and fry until browned. Add marinade and seasoning and bring to
the boil. Cover and simmer for 1
hour or until tender. Stir
occasionally.

3 Taste and adjust seasoning before serving garnished with
coriander sprigs.

Menu Suggestion
Serve with Iced Sorrel Soup
(page 11), Vegetable Pilau
(page 97) and Lemon Balm
Syllabub (page 105).

ROGAN JOSH

(INDIAN LAMB CURRY WITH TOMATOES AND YOGURT)

| 1.45 | £ £ ✳* | 287–430 cals |

* freeze after stage 2

Serves 4–6

45 ml (3 tbsp) vegetable oil

1 onion, skinned and sliced

3 garlic cloves, skinned and crushed

10 ml (2 tsp) ground ginger

10 ml (2 tsp) paprika

15 ml (1 tbsp) ground coriander

5 ml (1 tsp) ground cumin

5 ml (1 tsp) ground turmeric

2.5 ml ($\frac{1}{2}$ tsp) cayenne pepper

large pinch of ground cloves

large pinch of ground cardamom

700 g (1$\frac{1}{2}$ lb) boned lean lamb, (shoulder or leg), cubed

284 g (10 oz) natural yogurt

5 ml (1 tsp) salt

4 tomatoes, skinned and chopped

extra natural yogurt and lemon wedges, to garnish

1 Heat the oil in a large pan and brown the onion. Add the crushed garlic and spices with the meat and gently fry for 5 minutes.

2 Stir in the yogurt, salt and tomatoes. Bring to boil, cover and simmer, stirring occasionally, for about 1$\frac{1}{2}$ hours until the meat is tender and the sauce has thickened. If the sauce thickens too much before the meat is cooked add extra water or tomato juice.

3 Swirl yogurt over the top of the rogan josh and garnish with lemon wedges.

Menu Suggestion
Serve with Mulligatawny Soup (page 25), Sag Aloo (page 97) and Geranium Grape Sorbet (page 115).

SAUERBRATEN

| 2.30* | £ | ✳* | 691–1036 cals |

* plus 30 minutes cooling and 2–3
days marinating; freeze after stage 3

Serves 4–6

200 ml (⅓ pint) red wine

60 ml (4 tbsp) red wine vinegar

1 large onion, skinned and sliced

1 large carrot, peeled and sliced

1 bay leaf

1 sprig of fresh thyme

4 cloves

6 black peppercorns

15 ml (1 tbsp) dark soft brown sugar

5 ml (1 tsp) mustard powder

salt

1.5 kg (3–3½ lb) piece top rump or
     topside of beef, rolled and tied

50 g (2 oz) beef dripping or lard

45 ml (3 tbsp) plain flour

25 g (1 oz) butter or margarine,
     softened

about 90 ml (6 tbsp) soured cream

freshly ground pepper

1 Make the marinade. Put the
wine, vinegar, onion, carrot,
herbs, spices, sugar and mustard
in a pan with 5 ml (1 tbsp) salt.
Bring to the boil, stirring to
combine.

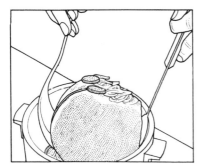

2 Put the beef in an earthenware
bowl or casserole. Pour over
the marinade and leave to cool
for 30 minutes, then cover and
marinate in the refrigerator for 2–3
days. Turn the beef occasionally
during this time.

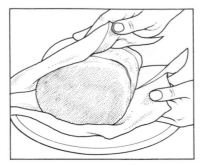

3 To cook the beef: lift the joint
out of the marinade and pat
dry with absorbent kitchen paper.
Melt dripping in a large casserole,
add beef and fry over brisk heat
for a few minutes until browned.
Lower heat, pour in marinade and
cover with a lid. Simmer for 2
hours or until the beef is tender.

4 Remove beef and keep warm.
Strain the cooking liquid, then
return to the casserole.

5 To make the *beurre manié*,
work the flour and butter to a
paste. Add paste to liquid a little
at a time, whisking over high heat
for a smooth, thick sauce.

6 Stir in the soured cream over
low heat; season. Serve sliced
with a little sauce poured over.

Menu Suggestion
Serve with Stuffed Tarragon
Tomatoes (page 20), Cabbage with
Caraway (page 99) and Spiced
Dried Fruit Compote (page 116).

SAUERBRATEN

Literally translated, *sauerbraten*
means 'sour beef' in German—
so called because the meat is
marinated in a mixture of wine
and vinegar for 2–3 days. This
long marinating time ensures
tender, moist beef, even with
such inexpensive cuts as topside.

There are numerous different
recipes for sauerbraten all over
Germany, some of which include
raisins in their ingredients, but
all have the same unique sweet-
sour flavour which comes from
the combination of sugar and
vinegar in the acid marinade.
The Germans like to serve sauerbraten for their main Sunday
meal, with noodles tossed in
butter and a dish of apple sauce
or stewed apple—and ice-cold
beer to drink.

Potato dumplings
These are a favourite accompaniment for those with hearty
appetites. To make sufficient
dumplings for 4–6 people, boil
450 g (1 lb) potatoes until
tender, then drain and mash well
until smooth. Add **1 beaten egg,
50 g (2 oz) fresh white breadcrumbs, 10 ml (2 tsp) cornflour,** and **freshly grated nutmeg, salt and freshly ground
pepper** to taste. Mix well together, then knead until smooth
and shape into 8–10 balls with
floured hands. Just before the
sauerbraten finishes cooking,
drop the dumplings into a pan of
boiling salted water and boil for
15 minutes until puffed up and
risen to the surface. Drain and
serve hot, with melted butter and
more freshly grated nutmeg, if
liked.

Porc Au Poivre
(PORK WITH PEPPERCORNS)

| 1.15 | £ | 463 cals |

Serves 6

30 ml (2 tbsp) fresh green pepper-corns or dried black peppercorns

6 large pork chops

50 g (2 oz) butter or margarine

566-g (20-oz) can pineapple slices

30 ml (2 tbsp) plain flour

90 ml (6 tbsp) dry sherry

salt

12 cooked prunes, drained and stoned

parsley sprigs, to garnish

1 If using dried peppercorns, crush in a pestle and mortar. Trim the chops of excess fat and brown well in the hot butter in a frying pan. Place side by side in a shallow ovenproof dish.

2 Drain the pineapple slices, re-serve juices and brown in residual fat. Spoon over chops.

3 Stir flour into pan with sherry, pineapple juice, peppercorns and salt and bring to the boil. Stir in prunes and spoon over chops. Cover the dish tightly and cook in the oven at 180°C (350°F) mark 4 for 50 minutes. Garnish and serve.

Menu Suggestion
Serve with Mussels with Garlic and Parsley (page 23) and Rhubarb and Orange Fool (page 111).

Sorrel Stuffed Lamb

| 3.00* | £ | ✳* | 605 cals |

* plus 30 minutes cooling; freeze after stuffing

Serves 6

15 ml (1 tbsp) vegetable oil

2 onions, skinned and finely chopped

450 g (1 lb) chopped fresh sorrel, washed and trimmed

1 garlic clove, skinned and crushed

2.5 ml ($\frac{1}{2}$ tsp) grated nutmeg

1.25 ml ($\frac{1}{4}$ tsp) ground allspice

salt and freshly ground pepper

1.4-kg (3-lb) boned leg of lamb

10 ml (2 tsp) flour

300 ml ($\frac{1}{2}$ pint) chicken stock

15 ml (1 tbsp) redcurrant jelly

dash of gravy browning

1 Heat the oil in a pan and cook onions for 10 minutes until soft and lightly coloured. Add the sorrel, garlic, nutmeg, allspice and seasoning, with plenty of pepper. Cook for a further 5 minutes. Cool for about 30 minutes.

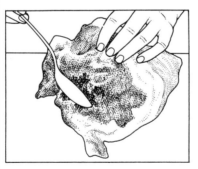

2 Using a large spoon, carefully fill the bone cavity of the leg of lamb with the cooled sorrel and onion mixture.

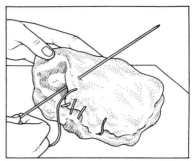

3 Sew up the lamb using a piece of cotton or fine string. Then place lamb on a rack in a roasting tin. Roast in the oven at 180°C (350°F) mark 4 for about 2$\frac{1}{2}$ hours. Baste several times during cooking.

4 Place the joint on a shallow serving plate, keep warm. Drain off all but 15 ml (1 tbsp) fat from the roasting tin, stir flour into pan, cook for 1–2 minutes. Add the stock, redcurrant jelly with seasoning and a dash of gravy browning; boil for 2–3 minutes stirring. Serve the gravy separately.

Menu Suggestion
Serve with Mussels with Garlic and Parsley (page 23) and Lemon Balm Syllabub (page 105).

SORREL
Sorrel is in fact a herb, although some people think of it as a vege-table just like spinach, which it closely resembles in appearance. There are two main types of sorrel—wild and French, and it is the latter which is best used in cooking, wild sorrel is rather too bitter.

Sorrel grows very easily in a sunny position in the garden, and it will grow all summer long if you pick it regularly. If you find the flavour a little sour, then use half sorrel and half spinach in this recipe.

LIVER AND BACON ROULADES

0.25*	£	226–301 cals

* plus 1 hour marinating

Serves 3–4

4 rashers streaky bacon, about 100 g (4 oz) total weight

225 g (8 oz) lamb's liver

60 ml (4 tbsp) orange juice

30 ml (2 tbsp) brandy

15 ml (1 tbsp) chopped fresh marjoram or oregano or 5 ml (1 tsp) dried

salt and freshly ground pepper

1 Cut the rind off each rasher and stretch the rashers with a blunt-edged knife. Cut each rasher across into three pieces.

2 Divide the liver into twelve even-sized pieces, removing any skin and ducts.

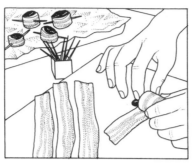

3 Roll a piece of bacon around each piece of liver and secure with a cocktail stick. Place in the base of a foil-lined grill pan.

4 Mix the orange juice, brandy, herbs and seasoning together and spoon over the bacon rolls. Leave to marinate in a cool place for 1 hour or longer.

5 Cook under a moderate grill for 12–15 minutes, turning and basting occasionally. Remove cocktail sticks before serving, replacing them with fresh ones if liked. Serve hot.

Menu Suggestion

Serve with Vegetable Pilau (page 97) and Spiced Dried Fruit Compote (page 116).

LIVER AND BACON ROULADES

The French word *roulade* means a roll or a rolled slice in culinary terms, and here it is used to describe the way in which bacon is rolled around pieces of lamb's liver. The method of marinating meat in a mixture of alcohol, fruit juice, herbs and seasonings is a very common one in French cookery—the purpose of a marinade is to tenderize the meat and make it flavoursome.

Some meats are left to marinate for as long as 2–3 days, but most marinades are left for an hour or so, overnight at the most. The combination of alcohol and an acid liquid such as juice from citrus fruit helps break down any tough fibres and sinews in meat, so it is a process which is well worth doing if it is specified in a recipe, especially if the meat is one of the inexpensive, tougher cuts. Any alcohol can be used, but red or white wine and brandy are popular.

Wine vinegar and lemon juice are the usual acid ingredients, although orange juice as specified in this recipe has much the same effect. Fresh pineapple juice is another popular marinade ingredient; it contains an enzyme which breaks down tough fibres in tough cuts of meat.

MADRAS BEEF CURRY

| 2.30 | £ | ✳ | 487 cals |

Serves 4

2.5-cm (1-inch) piece fresh root
  ginger, peeled

15 ml (1 tbsp) coriander seeds

10 ml (2 tsp) cumin seeds

10 ml (2 tsp) ground turmeric

10 ml (2 tsp) chilli powder

10 ml (2 tsp) garam masala (see
  page 156)

5 ml (1 tsp) salt

50 g (2 oz) ghee (see page 148) or
  vegetable oil

700–900 g (1½–2 lb) chuck steak, cut
  into bite-sized pieces

1 onion, skinned and thinly sliced

4 garlic cloves, skinned and
  roughly chopped

150 ml (¼ pint) water

1 Put the ginger, coriander and
cumin in a mortar and pestle
and pound to a paste. Add the
ground spices and the salt and mix
well together.

2 Melt the ghee in a heavy flameproof casserole, add the beef
and fry over moderate heat until
browned on all sides.

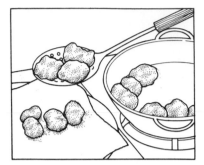

3 Remove the beef from the pan
with a slotted spoon and set
aside on absorbent kitchen paper.

4 Add the onion and garlic to
the pan, together with the spice
paste. Fry over gentle heat for 5
minutes, stirring constantly to prevent sticking and burning.

5 Return the beef to the pan and
stir to combine with the spice
mixture. Pour in the water and
bring to the boil, stirring.

6 Lower the heat, cover the pan
and simmer very gently for
1½–2 hours or until the beef is
tender. Before serving, taste and
add more salt if necessary.

Menu Suggestion
Serve with Sag Aloo (page 97)
and Sweet Indian Saffron Rice
(page 108).

MADRAS BEEF CURRY
The term 'Madras curry' is used
to describe any curry which is
hot, i.e. it will always contain a
fairly large quantity of chillies
or chilli powder. Madras curry
powder is available ready mixed
in drums and packets; while some
brands have a good flavour, it is
not a good idea to use them —
you will find that all your curries
tend to taste the same, and some
brands even taste stale. It is far
better to mix your own spices together as and when you need
them (see page 156).

The original recipe for a beef
curry such as this one would have
been developed by either the
Moslems or the Christians living
in southern India — the Hindus
of the north believe the cow is a
sacred animal and therefore never
eat beef.

As an alternative to beef, you
can use diced shoulder or leg of
lamb. You can also use chicken,
in which case you will need either
4 skinned portions or approximately the same weight of boneless chicken meat as given for the
beef in the recipe. Prawns also
taste good in a Madras curry —
use 450 g (1 lb) peeled prawns,
with 225 g (8 oz) sliced button
mushrooms to help make up the
weight if liked.

The traditional accompaniments to Madras curry in India
are plain white rice (basmati is
best) plus crisp poppadoms and a
hot lime pickle (available in jars
from Indian specialist shops and
some good supermarkets and
delicatessens). A mixed vegetable
curry or Sag Aloo (page 97)
would also make a suitable
accompaniment if you are
planning a full dinner party meal.
Serve ice-cold lager or beer to
drink, the spicy hotness of this
curry would be too strong for
any kind of wine.

RENDANG
(INDONESIAN SPICED BEEF WITH COCONUT)

| 1.30* | 🍳 | £ £ ✳ | 246 cals |

Serves 4

100 g (4 oz) block creamed coconut

300 ml (½ pint) boiling water

2 small onions, skinned and
  roughly chopped

2 garlic cloves, skinned and roughly
  chopped

5-cm (2-inch) piece fresh root
  ginger, peeled and roughly
  chopped

2–3 dried red chillies, according to
  taste, or 5 ml (1 tsp) chilli
  powder

5 ml (1 tsp) ground turmeric

5 ml (1 tsp) dried lemon grass
  (see page 138)

5 ml (1 tsp) laos powder (see page
  136)

700 g (1½ lb) top rump steak, cut
  into thick strips

5 ml (1 tsp) salt

lemon twists, to garnish

1 Make the coconut milk. Grate
the coconut into a heatproof
bowl, then pour in the boiling
water. Stir until the coconut has
dissolved, then strain through
cheesecloth or a fine wire sieve.

2 Make the paste. Put the onions,
garlic and ginger in an electric
blender or food processor with the
chillies, turmeric, lemon grass and
laos powder. Add about 30 ml (2
tbsp) of the coconut milk and work
to a thick paste.

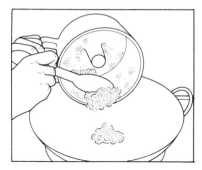

3 Transfer the paste to a wok or
deep, heavy frying-pan. Add
the steak and remaining coconut
milk, with the salt. Bring to the
boil, stirring constantly to combine
all the ingredients and prevent the
milk from curdling. Lower the
heat to moderate.

4 Simmer, uncovered, for about
1 hour until the meat is tender
and the sauce has reduced to a
thick, almost dry consistency, just
coating the meat.

5 At this stage the oil will have
separated out from the coconut
milk. Continue to cook over
moderate heat for a further 5–10
minutes so that the beef browns
in the oil. Stir constantly during
this cooking time to prevent sticking and burning. Taste and add
more salt if necessary. Garnish
with lemon twists before serving.

Menu Suggestion
Serve with Mulligatawny Soup
(page 25) and Geranium Grape
Sorbet (page 115).

RENDANG
This is a thick, spicy curry from
West Sumatra in Indonesia. It is
a favourite dish of the Minang-
kabau people who live in the
high hills there. Originally made
with buffalo meat, it is a dish
which was developed for its
keeping qualities—the meat is
cooked for a long time in spices
and *santen* (coconut milk made
from fresh coconut flesh) until it
turns very dark, which has the
effect of preserving it—even in
a tropical climate it is said to
be possible to keep rendang for
several weeks.

Rendang is therefore a good
dish to make in advance of a
party since it keeps and reheats
very well. Serve with prawn
crackers, fluffy boiled white rice,
pickles and chutneys. Ice-cold
lager is the ideal drink.

Rendang is a simple dish to
make, but it does need careful
watching and stirring most of the
time—this is because of the oil
present in the coconut milk. If
you like, you can make your own
coconut milk with grated fresh
coconut flesh (see page 157), but
creamed coconut available in a
block from supermarkets is a
quick, convenient substitute. Always strain it after dissolving,
however, and never cover the pan
while cooking or the gravy may
curdle. Cook the meat and coconut milk together until the oil
begins to run out of the sauce,
then continue cooking and
stirring so that the meat fries in
the oil—this is a very important
stage in the cooking of rendang,
and one that should not be
omitted even if you are short of
time.

PORK ESCALOPES WITH SAGE

0.20	£ ✳*	444 cals

* freeze at the end of stage 3

Serves 4

450 g (1 lb) pork fillet

1 egg, beaten

100 g (4 oz) fresh brown
   breadcrumbs

30 ml (2 tbsp) fresh sage or 10 ml
   (2 tsp) dried

grated rind of 1 lemon

75 g (3 oz) butter, melted

lemon wedges, to serve

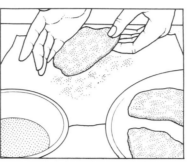

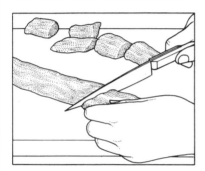

1 Using a sharp knife, trim any excess fat from the pork fillet and cut the meat into 5-mm ($\frac{1}{4}$-inch) slices.

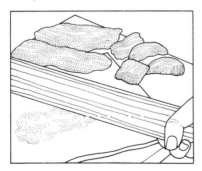

2 Beat out into even thinner slices between two sheets of greaseproof paper, using a meat cleaver or a wooden rolling pin.

3 Coat the escalopes with the beaten egg. Then mix together the breadcrumbs, sage and grated lemon rind and coat the pork escalopes.

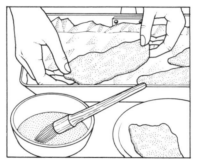

4 Lay in the base of a grill pan lined with foil (this quantity will need to be grilled in two batches). Brush with melted butter. Grill for about 3 minutes each side. Serve with lemon wedges.

Menu Suggestion
Serve with Stuffed Tarragon Tomatoes (page 20), Turnips in Curry Cream Sauce (page 100) and Spiced Dried Fruit Compote (page 116).

BOBOTIE
(SPICY MINCED LAMB PIE)

| 1.15 | ✳ | 457–685 cals |

Serves 4–6

1 thick slice of white bread, crusts
   removed

300 ml ($\frac{1}{2}$ pint) milk

25 g (1 oz) butter or margarine

1 large onion, skinned and chopped

2 eating apples, peeled and chopped

50 g (2 oz) seedless raisins, currants
   or sultanas

30 ml (2 tbsp) curry powder (see
   page 156)

5 ml (1 tsp) sugar

salt and freshly ground pepper

700 g ($1\frac{1}{2}$ lb) lean cooked minced
   lamb or beef

2 eggs

25 g (1 oz) flaked almonds

bay leaves, to garnish

1 Soak the bread in the milk for
a few minutes, then squeeze
the bread with your fingers, catch-
ing the milk in a bowl. Reserve
bread and milk separately.

2 Melt the butter in a
flameproof dish, add the
chopped onion and fry gently for 5
minutes until soft but not coloured.

3 Add the apples and raisins, the
curry powder, sugar and salt
and pepper to taste. Fry for a
further 2 minutes, stirring, then
add the lamb and the reserved
bread. Stir to combine. Remove
from the heat and level the surface.

4 Beat the eggs with the reserved
milk and salt and pepper to
taste. Pour slowly over the lamb,
and sprinkle over the almonds.
Cook in the oven at 180°C (350°F)
mark 4 for 45 minutes to 1 hour
until the custard is set. Serve hot
straight from the dish, garnished
with bay leaves.

Menu Suggestion
Serve with Vegetable Pilau
(page 97) and Poached Pears in
Ginger Syrup (page 114).

BOBOTIE
Bobotie is a traditional South
African dish, although the
original recipe came from the Far
East and it found its way to
South Africa via the Dutch!

   This may seem like a round-
about way for a recipe to turn up
in a particular country, but the
explanation is in fact very simple.
In 1652, the Dutch founded the
Cape, and spent the next 200
years bringing their Malay
servants from their colonies in
the Far East to work for them in
South Africa. Bobotie is one of
the many Malay recipes which
these servants brought with them
—and cooked for their masters.

   In this recipe, bay leaves are
used as a garnish, but in South
Africa the traditional garnish is
lemon leaves. Lemon trees grow
in abundance there, and they are
frequently used in cooking for
their tangy flavour. Bay leaves
look very similar, but unfor-
tunately their flavours are not at
all alike.

   If you prefer to use raw
minced beef or lamb rather than
the cooked meat specified in this
recipe, it will taste just as good,
but it will need to be cooked for
20 minutes in stage 3.

MAIN COURSES

Poultry and Game

Chicken, duck, turkey, pheasant and other game birds marry well with herbs and spices, and in this chapter you will find recipes both for everyday family meals, and for special dinner party main courses. Traditional British and French dishes alongside exotic concoctions from the East — turn the pages and you'll find you're spoilt for choice.

ROAST DUCK WITH SPICED STUFFING

| *2.30* | £ £ | 973 cals |

Serves 4

100 g (4 oz) Italian risotto rice, boiled and drained
100 g (4 oz) dried apricots, finely chopped
50 g (2 oz) pine kernels, roughly chopped
25 g (1 oz) seedless raisins
1 onion, skinned and finely chopped
2.5 ml ($\frac{1}{2}$ tsp) ground cinnamon
2.5 ml ($\frac{1}{2}$ tsp) freshly grated nutmeg
2.5 ml ($\frac{1}{2}$ tsp) ground cumin
salt and freshly ground pepper
2–2.5 kg (4–4$\frac{1}{2}$ lb) oven-ready duck
25 g (1 oz) butter
30 ml (2 tbsp) clear honey
watercress sprigs, to garnish
canned apricot halves, to serve (optional)

1 Make the stuffing. Combine the first eight ingredients together until well mixed, adding salt and pepper to taste.

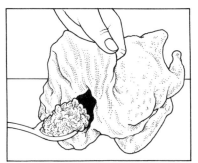

2 Wash the inside of the duck and pat dry with absorbent kitchen paper. Put the stuffing inside the neck end of duck, then truss with string and/or skewers.

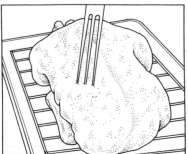

3 Melt the butter and honey together. Stand the duck on a rack in a roasting tin, then prick all over with a fork. Brush all over with the honey and butter and sprinkle liberally with salt and freshly ground pepper.

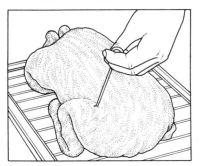

4 Roast the duck in the oven at 180°C (350°F) mark 4 for 1$\frac{1}{2}$–2 hours or until the flesh feels tender when pierced in the thick part of the thigh with a skewer. Serve hot, garnished with watercress sprigs, and warmed apricot halves filled with a little of the stuffing, if liked.

Menu Suggestion
Serve with Prawn and Dill Tartlets (page 21) and Poached Pears in Ginger Syrup (page 114).

HERBY GARLIC CHICKEN IN A BRICK

2.00	🎩	388 cals

Serves 4

6 garlic cloves, skinned

175 g (6 oz) unsalted butter, softened

30 ml (2 tbsp) chopped fresh tarragon or 10 ml (2 tsp) dried

finely grated rind of 1 lemon

salt and freshly ground pepper

1.75-kg (3½-lb) oven-ready roasting chicken

fresh tarragon, to garnish

1 Prepare the chicken brick according to instructions (see right). Crush four garlic cloves, then beat into 100 g (4 oz) of the butter with the tarragon, lemon rind and salt and pepper to taste. Cut the remaining two garlic cloves in half.

2 Put the four garlic halves inside the chicken and sprinkle with salt and freshly ground pepper.

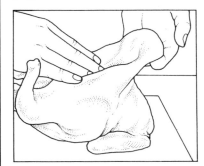

3 With your fingers, very carefully ease the breast skin of the chicken away from the flesh.

4 Using your fingers again, push the butter mixture in between the skin and the flesh of the bird, taking great care not to split the fragile skin over the breastbone.

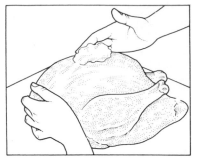

5 Spread the remaining butter over the outside of the skin, especially the legs.

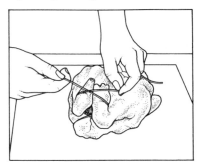

6 Sprinkle liberally with salt and pepper. Then truss the bird with string and/or skewers.

7 Remove the chicken brick from the water, place the chicken in the bottom and cover with the lid. Put in a cold oven and cook at 220°C (425°F) mark 7 for 1½ hours, without opening the oven door. Serve hot garnished with fresh tarragon.

Menu Suggestion

Serve with Iced Sorrel Soup (page 11) and Chocolate and Vanilla Roulade (page 113).

BRICK COOKERY

Baking meat and poultry in clay is one of the oldest of cooking methods, but it is only in recent years that the method has been revived and cooking vessels made of clay (called 'bricks') have become widely available in the shops. The principle behind the method of brick cookery is that meat or poultry is sealed in wet clay, making the meat moist and succulent.

All bricks are made of unglazed clay and are porous. Before using for the first time they should be treated or the food will taste of clay. Consult manufacturers' instructions or use one of the following methods:

1 Fill both halves of the brick with a mixture of water and vegetables such as celery, carrot and onion, then simmer over an asbestos mat for about 2 hours.

2 If you like the flavour of garlic, then rub the inside of the brick with cut peeled garlic cloves—the oil will act as a seal.

Each time you cook in the brick, it should be prepared beforehand by being left to soak in cold water for about 30 minutes. After soaking, drain the brick, then fill with meat or poultry according to individual recipe instructions. Put the lid on the brick, then place in a cold oven (this is very important—if the brick were to go straight into a hot oven it might crack). Turn the oven temperature to 220°C (425°F) mark 7 and cook, without opening the oven door, for the time specified in the recipe. After cooking and serving, rinse in a solution of water and vinegar until clean.

TANDOORI CHICKEN

| 2.15* | 361 cals |

* plus 5½ hours marinating

Serves 4

4 chicken quarters, skinned

30 ml (2 tbsp) lemon juice

1 garlic clove, skinned

2.5-cm (1-inch) piece fresh root ginger, peeled and chopped

1 green chilli, seeded

15 ml (1 tbsp) water

60 ml (4 tbsp) natural yogurt

5 ml (1 tsp) ground cumin

5 ml (1 tsp) garam masala (see page 156)

15 ml (1 tbsp) paprika

5 ml (1 tsp) salt

30 ml (2 tbsp) melted ghee (see page 148) or vegetable oil

shredded lettuce, lemon wedges and onion rings, to serve

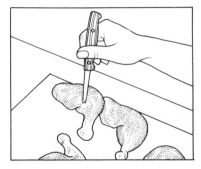

1 Using a sharp knife or skewer, pierce all the flesh of the chicken pieces.

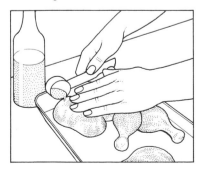

2 Put chicken in an ovenproof dish, add lemon juice; rub into flesh. Cover; leave for 30 minutes.

3 Make the marinade. Put the garlic, ginger and green chilli and water in an electric blender or food processor and grind to a smooth paste.

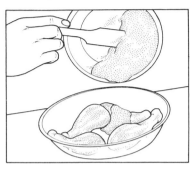

4 Add the paste to the yogurt, ground cumin, garam masala, paprika, salt and the melted ghee. Mix all the ingredients together, then pour them slowly over the chicken pieces.

5 Coat the pieces liberally with the yogurt marinade. Cover and leave to marinate at room temperature for 5 hours. Turn once or twice during this time.

6 Roast the chicken, uncovered, at 170°C (325°F) mark 3 for 1¾–2 hours, basting frequently and turning once, until tender and most of the marinade has evaporated. Alternatively, grill the chicken or barbecue, or roast it in a chicken brick. Serve with shredded lettuce, lemon wedges and onion rings.

Menu Suggestion

Serve with Mulligatawny Soup (page 25), Sag Aloo (page 97) and Geranium Grape Sorbet (page 115).

TANDOORI COOKING

The Indian *tandoor* is a clay oven, which is usually about 1 metre (3 feet) high, although some are as much as twice this height. At the base of the oven is a charcoal or wood fire which burns extremely fiercely so that searing temperatures are reached—small whole chickens can cook in a few minutes.

Although chicken is one of the most popular meats to be cooked in a *tandoor*, other kinds of meat, vegetables and bread are also cooked—*naan* bread, for example, is actually cooked on the wall of the oven at the same time as the meat and poultry are cooking on spits in the centre. To achieve exactly the same flavour as food cooked in a *tandoor* is virtually impossible in a conventional oven, but the tandoori marinade is almost as important as the cooking method, so with the correct marinade recipe you are nearly half-way there and cooking can be successfully done in a hot oven—or better still on a spit over a barbecue. All tandoori marinades are intended to tenderize and aromatise the food they cover, they differ slightly according to individual recipes, but most are based on yogurt, lemon juice, garlic, chillies and spices.

The orangey-red colour of tandoori food is achieved with food colouring—usually a mixture of red and yellow. You may or may not wish to use this, but it is worth experimenting to achieve an 'authentic' look.

Once the food is cooking the yogurt marinade will form a thick crust which helps seal in the meat's natural juices. Turn and baste the meat during cooking, but do not puncture the crust or the juices will run out, resulting in dry, flavourless meat.

TURKEY IN SPICED YOGURT

| 1.30* | 328 cals |

* plus overnight marinating

Serves 6

turkey leg on the bone, about 1.1 kg (2½ lb) in weight

7.5 ml (1½ tsp) ground cumin

7.5 ml (1½ tsp) ground coriander

2.5 ml (½ tsp) ground turmeric

2.5 ml (½ tsp) ground ginger

salt and freshly ground pepper

284 g (10 oz) natural yogurt

30 ml (2 tbsp) lemon juice

45 ml (3 tbsp) vegetable oil

225 g (8 oz) onions, skinned and sliced

45 ml (3 tbsp) desiccated coconut

30 ml (2 tbsp) plain flour

150 ml (¼ pint) chicken stock or water

chopped fresh parsley, to garnish

1 Cut the turkey meat off the bone into large fork-sized pieces, discarding the skin (there should be about 900 g [2 lb] meat).

2 Make the marinade. In a large bowl mix the spices with the seasoning, yogurt and lemon juice. Stir well until evenly blended. Fold through the turkey meat until coated with the yogurt mixture. Cover tightly with cling film and refrigerate overnight.

3 Heat the oil in a medium flameproof casserole, add the onion and fry for about 5 minutes until lightly brown. Add the coconut and flour and fry gently, stirring for about 1 minute.

4 Off the heat stir in the turkey with its marinade, and the stock. Return to the heat and bring slowly to the boil, stirring all the time to prevent sticking.

5 Cover tightly and cook in the oven at 170°C (325°F) mark 3 for 1–1¼ hours or until the turkey is tender when tested with a fork. To serve, adjust the seasoning and serve garnished with parsley.

Menu Suggestion

Serve with Pork Pâté with Sage and Juniper Berries (page 19) and Summer Fruit Salad (page 106).

YOGURT

Plain unsweetened yogurt is used extensively in Indian and Middle Eastern cooking for many reasons. It is often used as a marinade as in this recipe, because it has the effect of tenderizing meat—it contains certain live bacteria which help break down tough fibres and sinews, making the meat more succulent and juicy when cooked.

Plain yogurt is also used to offset the hotness of chillies and the rawness of spices. For this reason it can be combined with the other ingredients as here, although it is often served as a side dish for people to help themselves whenever they feel a dish is too hot for their liking. It is for this same reason that Indians often drink yogurt when eating curry—to counteract the heat of the food, refresh the palate and aid digestion. Called *lassi*, this yogurt drink is made by diluting yogurt with water then whisking it until frothy.

CHICKEN WITH TARRAGON SAUCE

0.30	346 cals

Serves 6

6 chicken breasts, skinned

75 g (3 oz) butter or margarine

25 g (1 oz) plain flour

450 ml (¾ pint) chicken stock

30 ml (2 tbsp) tarragon vinegar

10 ml (2 tsp) French mustard

5 ml (1 tsp) fresh chopped tarragon or 2.5 ml (½ tsp) dried

45 ml (3 tbsp) grated Parmesan cheese

salt and freshly ground pepper

150 ml (5 fl oz) single cream

tarragon sprigs, to garnish

1 In a covered pan, slowly fry the chicken breasts in 50 g (2 oz) butter for about 20 minutes until tender, turning once.

2 Meanwhile, melt the remaining butter in a pan, stir in the flour and gradually add the stock and vinegar. Stir in the mustard, tarragon and cheese; bring to the boil. Season with salt and pepper, simmer for 3 minutes.

3 Remove from the heat and add the cream. Heat gently without boiling. To serve, place the drained chicken on a serving dish, spoon over the sauce and garnish.

Menu Suggestion
Serve with Prawn and Dill Tartlets (page 21) and Poached Pears in Ginger Syrup (page 114).

TARRAGON VINEGAR
Why not make your own tarragon vinegar for this recipe? You will find it immensely useful for other recipes too, and it keeps its flavour well for many months. Use it in marinades for poultry and fish—and in salad dressings. Follow the recipe for Herb Vinegar on page 154, using fresh tarragon sprigs.

RABBIT CASSEROLE WITH SAGE DUMPLINGS

| 2.15 | ✳* | 481 cals |

* freeze without dumplings

Serves 4

100 g (4 oz) bacon, rinds removed

4 rabbit portions

4 sticks celery, chopped

2 leeks, trimmed and sliced

1 bay leaf

225 g (8 oz) carrots, sliced

30 ml (2 tbsp) plain flour

600 ml (1 pint) chicken stock

salt and freshly ground pepper

75 g (3 oz) self-raising flour

40 g (1½ oz) shredded suet

5 ml (1 tsp) chopped fresh sage or 2.5 ml (½ tsp) dried

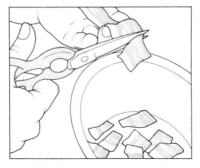

1 Using a sharp pair of kitchen scissors, snip the bacon into a flameproof casserole. Fry for 5 minutes until the fat runs. Add the rabbit and fry gently, then add celery, leeks, bay leaf and carrots.

2 Sprinkle over the plain flour and stir well. Now add the stock a little at a time and bring to the boil, stirring. Season to taste.

3 Cover the casserole and cook in the oven at 170°C (325°F) mark 3 for about 1½ hours or until the rabbit is tender.

4 Make the dumpling dough. Combine the self-raising flour, shredded suet, sage and salt and freshly ground pepper. Mix to a soft dough with cold water.

5 Divide the dough into four portions, then shape evenly into balls and place on top of casserole. Cover again and cook for 20–25 minutes until dumplings are well risen and cooked through.

Menu Suggestion
Serve with Peppered Carrots (page 98) and creamed potatoes.

CHICKEN WITH SAFFRON

| 1.15 | 🍴 | 316 cals |

Serves 6

6 chicken breasts about 175 g (6 oz)
   each
30 ml (2 tbsp) plain flour
salt and freshly ground pepper
40 g (1½ oz) butter
200 ml (⅓ pint) chicken stock
30 ml (2 tbsp) dry white wine
large pinch of saffron strands
2 egg yolks
60 ml (4 tbsp) single cream
vegetable julienne, to garnish

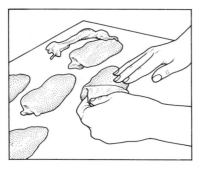

1 Skin the chicken breasts and
remove any fat. Lightly coat
the chicken in the flour, seasoned
with salt and pepper.

2 Melt the butter in a medium
flameproof casserole. Fry the
chicken pieces, half at a time, for
5–10 minutes until golden brown.

3 Return all the chicken pieces
to the pan with any remaining
flour and pour in the chicken stock
and white wine.

4 Sprinkle in the saffron, push-
ing it down under the liquid.
Bring up to the boil, cover tightly,
and bake in the oven at 180°C
(350°F) mark 4 for about 50 minutes until cooked.

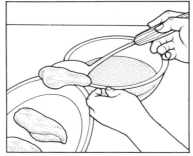

5 Lift the chicken out of the
juices and place in an edged
serving dish. Cover and keep
warm in a low oven.

6 Strain the cooking juices into a
small saucepan. Mix the egg
yolks and cream together and off
the heat stir into the cooking
juices until evenly mixed.

7 Cook gently, stirring all the
time until the juices thicken
slightly. Do not boil. To serve,
adjust seasoning, spoon over the
chicken and garnish with
vegetable julienne. Serve
immediately.

Menu Suggestion
Serve with Shamee Kebab with
Yogurt Mint Dip (page 24) and
Spiced Dried Fruit Compote
(page 116).

GAME PIE

2.45 | £ ✳* | 602–903 cals

* freeze after stage 5

Serves 4–6

| 450 g (1 lb) boned game (e.g. pigeon, venison, partridge, hare or pheasant) |
| 30 ml (2 tbsp) plain flour, for coating |
| 10 ml (2 tsp) dried thyme |
| 2.5 ml ($\frac{1}{2}$ tsp) ground cinnamon |
| salt and freshly ground pepper |
| 45 ml (3 tbsp) vegetable oil |
| 300 ml ($\frac{1}{2}$ pint) red wine |
| 6 juniper berries, lightly crushed |
| 350 g (12 oz) pork sausagemeat |
| 225 g (8 oz) packet frozen puff pastry, thawed |
| 1 beaten egg, to glaze |

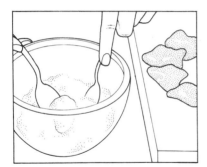

1 Cut the meat into even-sized cubes, then toss in the flour mixed with the thyme, cinnamon and seasoning.

2 Heat the oil in a flameproof casserole, add the meat and fry over moderate heat for 5 minutes until browned on all sides. Pour in the wine, add the juniper berries, then cover and simmer gently for 1–1$\frac{1}{2}$ hours until tender. Leave until cold, preferably overnight.

3 Put half the sausagemeat in the bottom of an ovenproof pie dish. Put the game mixture on top, then cover with the remaining sausagemeat and level the surface.

4 Roll out the dough on a floured surface and cut a thin strip long enough to go around the rim of the pie dish. Moisten the rim with water, then place the strip on the rim.

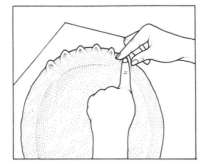

5 Roll out the remaining dough for a lid, moisten the strip of dough, then place the lid on top and press to seal. Knock up and flute the edge, and use pastry trimmings to make decorations for the top of the pie, sticking them on with water.

6 Brush the pastry with beaten egg, then bake in the oven at 200°C (400°F) mark 6 for 30 minutes until golden brown and crisp. Leave to stand for 15 minutes before serving, or serve cold.

Menu Suggestion
Serve with Cabbage with Caraway (page 99) and roast or jacket-baked potatoes.

GAME
When buying game for a casserole or pie such as this one, it is not necessary to buy young, small birds (these are best reserved for roasting). Ask your dealer for an older bird, which should be less expensive.

Fresh venison is excellent meat for casseroles and pies, since certain cuts such as shoulder benefit from long, slow cooking, and they are not too expensive. It is only in season for a short time, but some supermarkets sell frozen venison out of season which is ready cut up. This—and cubed hare and rabbit (which is not strictly speaking game)—is usually a good buy for pies and casseroles.

All game bought from a licensed dealer will have been hung for the appropriate length of time (to tenderize the flesh and intensify the 'gamey' flavour), so you will not have to worry about this—or plucking and drawing. Carefully remove the raw flesh from the carcass, then cut into bite-sized pieces. You will need approximately 4 pigeons, 2–3 partridges or 1–2 pheasants to obtain 450 g (1 lb) boneless meat for the game pie recipe on this page. Venison can be simply cut up like stewing steak; hare and rabbit joints should be boned and cut up as for chicken portions. If using frozen game, it should be defrosted before cooking—allow a full 24 hours in the refrigerator.

ROAST PHEASANT WITH HERBY FORCEMEAT BALLS

1.15	£ £	860 cals

Serves 4

2 young pheasants, plucked and drawn

150 g (5 oz) butter

10 ml (2 tsp) dried thyme

salt and freshly ground pepper

4 rashers of smoked streaky bacon

450 ml (¾ pint) giblet or chicken stock

225 g (8 oz) pork sausagemeat

50 g (2 oz) fresh white breadcrumbs

finely grated rind of ½ a lemon

25 g (1 oz) shredded suet

15 ml (1 tbsp) chopped fresh parsley

15 ml (1 tbsp) chopped fresh lemon thyme, or 10 ml (2 tsp) dried

15 ml (1 tbsp) chopped fresh sage

1 onion, skinned and finely chopped

1 egg, beaten

1 Wash the inside of the pheasants, then dry with absorbent kitchen paper. Put 15 g (½ oz) butter and 5 ml (1 tsp) thyme inside each bird. Season the birds inside with salt and pepper, then truss with string and/or skewers.

2 Brush the breast of each bird with 25 g (1 oz) softened butter and sprinkle with salt and pepper.

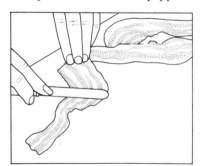

3 Stretch the bacon rashers with the flat of a knife blade, then use two rashers to cover each pheasant breast.

4 Stand the pheasants on a rack in a roasting tin, then pour the stock under the rack. Roast in the oven at 200°C (400°F) mark 6 for 25 minutes.

5 Meanwhile, make the herby forcemeat balls. Mix the sausagemeat, breadcrumbs, grated lemon rind, suet and herbs together until well combined.

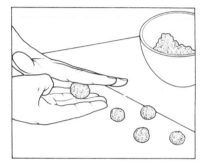

6 Melt 50 g (2 oz) butter in a small pan, add the onion and fry gently for 5 minutes until soft. Mix into the sausagemeat, add salt and pepper to taste, then bind with the beaten egg. Form the mixture into small balls by rolling it in your hands.

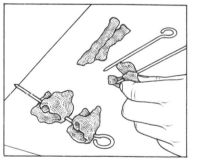

7 Remove the bacon rashers from the pheasants, roll them up and pierce them on to small metal skewers. Arrange on the rack around the pheasants, together with the forcemeat balls.

8 Return to the oven and roast for a further 20 minutes until the pheasants feel tender when pierced in the thickest part of the thighs with a skewer. Serve hot, with gravy made from the stock.

Menu Suggestion
Serve with Mulligatawny Soup (page 25), Cabbage with Caraway (page 99) and Hot Beetroot with Horseradish (page 101).

PHEASANT

Only young pheasants are suitable for roasting if the meat is to be tender and moist. Fresh birds are usually sold in a brace, i.e. one cock and one hen together. The cock is the most handsome of the two birds, with his long sweeping tail, green and rust plumage and bright green head crest. The hen pheasant is rather a dull brown, and smaller in size. When looking for young birds, check that the breast is firm and rounded and that the feathers are smooth, with tender wing tips. Check also that the legs are smooth and feet supple; the spurs should have rounded ends—long, sharp spurs are a sign of age.

Frozen pheasants are ready for cooking after defrosting—allow a full 24 hours in the refrigerator—but a fresh pheasant will need hanging, plucking, drawing and trussing beforehand—ask your dealer or butcher to do this for you. If you are going to stuff the bird, as in this recipe, then he can omit the trussing as you will have to do this after the bird has been stuffed.

When serving a brace of pheasant for 4 people, remember to give each person meat from both birds—the hen has moister flesh with a more delicate flavour than the cock.

Traditional accompaniments to roast pheasant are game chips, redcurrant jelly, brussels sprouts and chestnuts and bread sauce.

GINGERED JAPANESE CHICKEN

| 1.00 | 🍲 | £ | 361 cals |

Serves 4

1.4-kg (3-lb) oven-ready chicken
15 ml (1 tbsp) plain flour
15 ml (1 tbsp) ground ginger
60 ml (4 tbsp) vegetable oil
1 onion, skinned and sliced
283-g (10-oz) can bamboo shoots
1 red pepper, halved, seeded and
    sliced
150 ml ($\frac{1}{4}$ pint) chicken stock
45 ml (3 tbsp) soy sauce
45 ml (3 tbsp) medium dry sherry
salt and freshly ground pepper
100 g (4 oz) mushrooms, sliced

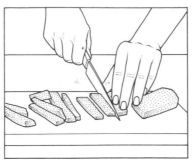

4 Cut up the canned bamboo shoots into 1-cm ($\frac{1}{2}$-inch) strips; add to the pan, together with the sliced pepper. Then stir in stock, soy sauce, sherry and seasoning. Bring to boil, cover, simmer 15 minutes.

5 Add the sliced mushrooms, cover again with lid and cook for a further 5–10 minutes, or until the chicken is tender.

Menu Suggestion
Serve with Spicy Crab Dip (page 13) and Rhubarb and Orange Fool (page 111).

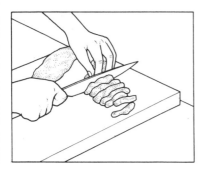

1 Cut all the flesh off the chicken and slice into chunky 'fingers', discarding the skin.

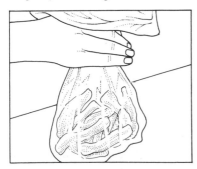

2 Mix the flour and ginger together in a polythene bag and toss the chicken in it to coat.

3 Heat the oil in a very large sauté or deep frying pan and fry the chicken and sliced onion together for 10–15 minutes until they are both golden.

BAMBOO SHOOTS

These are used extensively in oriental cooking, although the Chinese and Japanese use fresh shoots rather than the canned ones specified in this recipe. If fresh bamboo shoots are not obtainable, buy canned ones which are available at oriental specialist stores, large supermarkets and delicatessens. These make a very convenient substitute—they are pre-cooked, so all they need is draining and heating through.

The flavour of bamboo shoots is very difficult to describe. Some say they taste like mild asparagus, although asparagus afficionadoes would probably disagree! Look for those canned in water rather than those canned in vinegar—they will have a milder flavour.

MAIN COURSES

Fish and Shellfish

Herbs and spices lend themselves beautifully to the subtle, sometimes delicate flavours of fish and shellfish, but they should be used sparingly. Follow the quantities given in the recipes in this chapter accurately, or you can easily swamp the flavour of the fish itself.

SCALLOPS IN CREAMY BASIL SAUCE

| 0.25 | 🍳 | £ £ | 457 cals |

Serves 4

900 g (2 lb) shelled scallops, defrosted if frozen

30 ml (2 tbsp) vegetable oil

15 g ($\frac{1}{2}$ oz) butter

1 small onion, skinned and finely chopped

2 garlic cloves, skinned and crushed

150 ml ($\frac{1}{4}$ pint) dry white wine

20 ml (4 tsp) chopped fresh basil

salt and freshly ground pepper

150 ml (5 fl oz) double cream

few fresh basil sprigs, to garnish

5 Remove the scallops from the liquid with a slotted spoon and set aside on a plate. Boil the liquid until reduced by about half, then stir in the cream a little at a time and simmer until the sauce is thick.

6 Return the scallops to the pan and heat gently. To serve, taste and adjust the seasoning, and serve garnished with basil sprigs.

Menu Suggestion
Serve with Iced Sorrel Soup (page 11) and Geranium Grape Sorbet (page 115).

1 Cut the scallops (including the coral) into fairly thick slices. Pat dry with absorbent kitchen paper and set aside.

2 Heat the oil and butter in a large frying pan, add the onion and garlic and fry gently for 5 minutes until soft and lightly coloured.

3 Add the scallops to the pan and toss to coat in the oil and butter. Stir in the wine, basil and salt and pepper to taste.

4 Fry the scallops over moderate heat for 10 minutes until they are tender, turning them constantly so that they cook evenly on all sides. Do not overcook or they will become tough and rubbery.

SCALLOPS
One of the prettiest of shellfish, fresh scallops are sold in their delicately-coloured, fan-shaped shells. Frozen scallops, now available at high–class fish-mongers, are sold off the shell, but your fishmonger will let you have shells for serving if you ask him. Scald them in boiling water and scrub them before use.

Scallops are amongst the most expensive of shellfish, but their rich creaminess means a small amount goes a long way. The beautiful dark pink coral is considered a great delicacy. If you still feel they are extravagant, use half the quantity specified in this recipe and make up the weight with white button mushrooms.

HADDOCK AND CARAWAY CHEESE SOUFFLÉ

| 1.20 | 466 cals |

Serves 4

450 g (1 lb) floury potatoes

450 g (1 lb) fresh haddock fillets

100 g (4 oz) button mushrooms, wiped and thinly sliced

300 ml ($\frac{1}{2}$ pint) milk

1 bay leaf

25 g (1 oz) butter

25 g (1 oz) plain flour

2.5 ml ($\frac{1}{2}$ tsp) caraway seeds

125 g (4 oz) mature Cheddar cheese, grated

2 eggs, separated

salt and freshly ground pepper

1 Scrub the potatoes, boil until tender. Drain and peel, then mash three-quarters of the potatoes. Grate the remaining quarter into a bowl and set aside.

2 Meanwhile, place the haddock, mushrooms, milk and bay leaf in a small saucepan. Cover and poach for 15–20 minutes until tender. Drain, reserving milk and mushrooms. Flake fish, discarding skin and bay leaf.

3 Make the sauce. Melt the butter in a pan, stir in the flour and cook gently for 1 minute, stirring. Remove from the heat, add the caraway seeds and gradually stir in the milk. Bring to the boil, stirring, and simmer for 2–3 minutes until thickened and smooth.

4 Stir the mashed potato into the sauce with 75 g (3 oz) cheese, the egg yolks, fish and mushrooms. Season well.

5 Stiffly whisk the egg whites. Fold into the fish mixture. Turn into a 1.6-litre ($2\frac{3}{4}$-pint) buttered soufflé dish.

6 Sprinkle over the reserved grated potato and remaining grated cheese. Bake in the oven at 190°C (375°F) mark 5 for about 1 hour or until just set and golden brown.

Menu Suggestion
Serve with Chocolate and Vanilla Roulade (page 113).

TIPS FOR MAKING HOT SOUFFLÉS

● Always make sure to use the exact size of soufflé dish specified in the recipe.

● Check your oven temperature carefully and don't be tempted to bake a soufflé at a different temperature from the one specified.

● Preheat oven and baking sheet to required temperature well before baking.

● Fold egg whites in with a large metal spoon in a figure of eight motion so that the maximum amount of air is incorporated.

● Don't open the oven door during baking.

● Serve *immediately*—have your guests seated at the table well before the soufflé is due to come out of the oven.

STUFFED PLAICE WITH LEMON SAUCE

0.50	🍴 🍴	£ £	232 cals

Serves 4

4 small whole plaice, cleaned

65 g (2½ oz) butter

100 g (4 oz) button mushrooms, finely chopped

100 g (4 oz) white breadcrumbs

90 ml (6 tbsp) chopped parsley

45 ml (3 tbsp) green peppercorns, crushed

finely grated rind and juice of 2 lemons

1.25 ml (¼ tsp) mustard powder

salt and freshly ground pepper

1 egg, beaten

150 ml (¼ pint) dry white wine

25 g (1 oz) plain flour

150 ml (¼ pint) water

60 ml (4 tbsp) single cream

lemon slices and parsley sprigs, to garnish

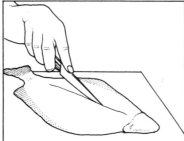

1 With the white skin uppermost, cut down the backbone of each of the four plaice.

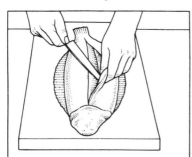

2 Carefully make a pocket on each side of the backbone by easing white flesh from bone.

3 Make the stuffing. Beat 15 g (½ oz) butter until softened then add the mushrooms, breadcrumbs, parsley, 30 ml (2 tbsp) peppercorns, lemon rind, mustard and salt and pepper to taste. Mix well and moisten with the egg and a little of the lemon juice.

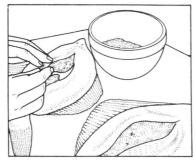

4 Spoon the stuffing carefully into the pockets in the fish. Then place the fish in a single layer in a buttered ovenproof dish. Pour the wine around the fish and cover loosely with foil. Cook in the oven at 190°C (375°F) mark 5 for 30 minutes.

5 Remove the fish from the dish and place on a warmed serving dish. Cover and keep warm in the oven turned to its lowest setting.

6 Make the sauce. Melt the remaining butter in a pan, add flour and stir over low heat for 1–2 minutes. Gradually stir in the fish cooking juices, the water and the remaining lemon juice. Bring to the boil, stirring, then lower the heat and stir in the remaining peppercorns and the cream.

7 To serve, taste and adjust the seasoning, then pour into a warmed sauceboat. Garnish the fish and serve at once, with the sauce handed separately.

Menu Suggestion
Serve with Deep-Fried Mushrooms with Herby Dressing (page 12) and Sweet Indian Saffron Rice (page 108).

FRICASSÉE OF MONKFISH WITH CORIANDER

| 0.40 | £ £ | 288 cals |

Serves 6

700 g (1½ lb) monkfish fillets

450 g (1 lb) halibut cutlets

150 ml (¼ pint) dry vermouth

300 ml (½ pint) water

1 small onion, skinned and sliced

salt and freshly ground pepper

125 g (4 oz) small button
    mushrooms, wiped

40 g (1½ oz) butter

45 ml (3 tbsp) plain flour

30 ml (2 tbsp) chopped fresh
    coriander and sprigs to garnish

60 ml (4 tbsp) single cream

1 Cut the monkfish and halibut into large, fork-sized pieces, discarding skin and bone.

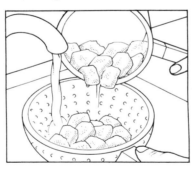

2 Place the fish in a medium saucepan, cover with cold water and bring slowly to the boil. Strain fish in a colander and then rinse off any scum.

3 Return the fish to the clean pan and pour over the vermouth with the 300 ml (½ pint) water. Add the onion with seasoning and bring to the boil. Cover the pan, reduce heat, and simmer gently for 8–10 minutes or until the fish is just tender and beginning to flake.

4 Add the mushrooms after 6 minutes of the cooking time. Strain off the cooking liquor and reserve for the sauce.

5 Melt the butter in a separate saucepan and stir in the flour followed by the cooking liquor. Bring slowly to the boil, stirring all the time, and bubble for 2 minutes until thickened and smooth.

6 Stir in the coriander, cream, mushrooms, onion and fish and adjust seasoning. Warm through gently, being careful not to break up the fish. Serve hot, garnished with sprigs of coriander.

Menu Suggestion

Serve with Blue Cheese Croquettes (page 84) and Geranium Grape Sorbet (page 115).

MONKFISH

Most good fishmongers stock monkfish nowadays, although it hasn't always been a popular fish because of its ugly appearance when whole. For this reason it is almost always displayed without the head, which is its ugliest part, and many fishmongers also skin and fillet it before offering it for sale. Monkfish fillets and steaks taste very like lobster and scampi, however, at a fraction of the price.

Monkfish has always been popular in Mediterranean countries, particularly Spain where it is called *rape* and France where it is known as *lotte de mer* or *baudroie*. The Spanish like to serve it cold in the same way as lobster, or hot with potatoes and tomatoes; the French braise it in white wine or serve it *en brochette* (on skewers).

SEAFOOD SAFFRON RISOTTO

| 0.45 | ☐ | £ £ | 488–732 cals |

Serves 4–6

good pinch of saffron strands

150 ml (¼ pint) boiling water

45 ml (3 tbsp) olive oil

30 ml (2 tbsp) butter or margarine

1 onion, skinned and chopped

2 garlic cloves, skinned and
  crushed

½ green pepper, finely chopped

½ red pepper, finely chopped

400 g (14 oz) Italian risotto rice

about 600 ml (1 pint) hot fish or
  chicken stock

120 ml (8 tbsp) dry white wine

1 bay leaf

salt and freshly ground pepper

350–450 g (¾–1 lb) frozen shelled
  scampi or jumbo prawns,
  thawed and thoroughly drained
  and dried

24 cooked mussels, shelled

a few mussels in shells, to garnish

freshly grated Parmesan cheese,
  to serve

1 Prepare the saffron water.
Soak the saffron strands in the
150 ml (¼ pint) boiling water for at
least 30 minutes.

2 Meanwhile, heat the oil and
half the butter in a heavy-
based pan, add the onion, garlic
and peppers and fry gently for 5
minutes until soft.

3 Add the rice and stir until
coated in the oil and butter.
Pour in a few spoonfuls of the
stock and the wine, then add the
saffron liquid.

4 Add the bay leaf and salt and
pepper to taste and simmer
gently, stirring frequently, until all
the liquid is absorbed by the rice.

5 Add a few more spoonfuls of
stock and simmer again until it
is absorbed. Continue adding
stock in this way for about 15
minutes, stirring frequently until
the rice is *al dente* (tender but firm
to the bite).

6 Melt the remaining butter in a
separate pan, add the scampi
and toss gently for about 5 minutes
until they change colour.

7 Remove the bay leaf from the
risotto, then stir in the scampi
and juices and the mussels. Warm
through, taste and adjust seasoning. Turn into a warmed serving
dish. Top with whole mussels and
serve at once with grated Parmesan
cheese handed separately.

Menu Suggestion
Serve with Mulligatawny Soup
(page 25) or Iced Sorrel Soup
(page 11) and Lemon Balm
Syllabub (page 105).

HOW TO MAKE AN AUTHENTIC RISOTTO

An Italian risotto is quite unlike
any other rice dish in consistency
—it is creamy and moist (the
Italians call this *all'onda*) and the
grains of rice tend to stick together unlike the fluffy individual grains of an Indian pilau,
for example. The reasons for this
are the type of rice used, and the
method of incorporating the
liquid, both of which are in-
credibly important if the risotto
is to look and taste authentic.

Italian risotto rice has a
rounded grain (but not so
rounded as pudding rice); it is
available in supermarkets in
boxes labelled 'Italian risotto
rice', but the best risotto rice to
buy are *avorio* and *arborio*, both
of which are available loose at
Italian delicatessens.

When making a risotto, follow
the instructions in the method
carefully, adding the liquid a
little at a time as in this recipe.
The rice should absorb each
amount of liquid before you add
the next, therefore it is really
a case of standing over it and
stirring and adding liquid almost
constantly until the correct consistency is obtained. Don't worry
if you do not need to add all the
liquid specified in a recipe—this
will depend on the type of rice
used, the quantity of other ingredients and the cooking temperature.

In Italy, risotto is always
served on its own before the
main course of fish or meat, but
it can of course be served as a
meal in itself, accompanied by
fresh crusty bread, a salad and a
bottle of chilled white wine—a
dry Soave or Frascati would go
well with the seafood in this
risotto.

TARRAGON STUFFED TROUT

1.30	🥘 £ £	320 cals

Serves 6

25 g (1 oz) long-grain rice

100 g (4 oz) peeled prawns

225 g (8 oz) button mushrooms, wiped

100 g (4 oz) onion, skinned

50 g (2 oz) butter

5 ml (1 tsp) chopped fresh tarragon or 1.25 ml (¼ tsp) dried

salt and freshly ground pepper

30 ml (2 tbsp) lemon juice

6 whole trout, about 225 g (8 oz) each, cleaned

tarragon sprigs, to garnish

1 Make the stuffing. Cut up each of the peeled prawns into two or three pieces. Boil the rice until tender; drain.

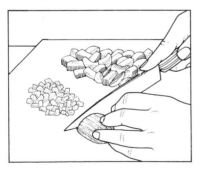

2 Roughly chop the mushrooms and finely chop the onion. Melt the butter in a large frying pan, add the onion and fry for 5 minutes until golden brown.

3 Add the mushrooms with the tarragon and seasoning and cook over high heat for 5–10 minutes until all excess moisture has evaporated. Cool for about 30 minutes.

4 Mix the prawns, rice, lemon juice and mushroom mixture together and season with salt and freshly ground pepper to taste.

5 Place the fish side by side in a lightly buttered oven-proof dish and stuff with the mixture. Cover and cook in the oven at 180°C (350°F) mark 4 for about 30 minutes. To serve, garnish the fish with sprigs of tarragon.

Menu Suggestion

Serve with Iced Sorrel Soup (page 11) and Summer Fruit Salad (page 106).

TYPES OF TROUT

When buying the fish for this recipe, choose between salmon trout and rainbow trout—both are available in suitable sizes for stuffing, although salmon trout can be as large as true salmon, so check carefully with your fish-monger first. Both are members of the salmon family, although the salmon trout, also called the sea trout because it spends the major part of its life at sea, is the closest to the salmon or 'king of the river'.

Fresh salmon trout are in season from early to mid summer, but frozen fish can be bought at other times of year. The flesh of salmon trout is a pretty, delicate shade of pink when cooked—similar to that of true salmon. Because it is less expensive than salmon it is a popular substitute in recipes calling for salmon.

For this recipe, rainbow trout is ideal. A freshwater fish, rainbow trout is now reared in large quantities on trout farms, and so is available all year round—fresh at fishmongers, chilled or frozen from supermarkets.

It is easily recognisable by its attractive silver skin and the shimmer of pink running down the centre of the fish from head to tail. The flesh of rainbow trout is pale and creamy in colour when cooked, the texture is soft and smooth, and the flavour very delicate.

Other kinds of trout which can be used for this recipe include grilse (a salmon which has only spent one year at sea before re-turning to spawn in fresh water) or brown or red trout.

SEAFOOD CURRY

| *0.30* | 361 cals |

Serves 4

1 fresh green chilli
45 ml (3 tbsp) vegetable oil
2 onions, skinned and sliced into
   rings
25 g (1 oz) desiccated coconut
15 ml (1 tbsp) plain flour
5 ml (1 tsp) ground coriander
450 g (1 lb) fresh haddock fillet,
   skinned and cut into chunks
150 ml ($\frac{1}{4}$ pint) white wine
25 g (1 oz) salted peanuts
125 g (4 oz) frozen prawns, thawed,
   drained and thoroughly dried
salt and freshly ground pepper
coriander sprigs and shredded
   coconut, toasted, to garnish

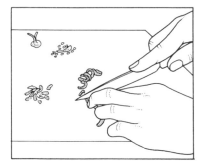

1 Halve the chilli, remove seeds and finely chop the flesh. Heat the oil in a large sauté pan, and brown the onion rings.

2 Mix coconut, flour and coriander and toss with the haddock and chopped chilli. Add to pan and fry gently for 5–10 minutes until golden, stirring.

3 Pour in wine, bring to boil and add peanuts, prawns and seasoning. Cover tightly and simmer for 5–10 minutes or until fish is tender. To serve, garnish with coriander and coconut.

Menu Suggestion
Serve with half quantity of Egg Mousse (page 88) and Lemon Balm Syllabub (page 105).

SKATE WITH CAPERS AND BLACK BUTTER

| 0.20 | 290 cals |

Serves 4

700–900 g (1½–2 lb) wing of skate

salt

50 g (2 oz) butter

15 ml (1 tbsp) white wine vinegar

10 ml (2 tsp) capers

10 ml (2 tsp) chopped fresh parsley, to garnish

1 Simmer the fish in salted water for 10–15 minutes until tender, drain and keep warm.

2 Heat the butter in a pan until lightly browned. Add the vinegar and capers, cook for a further 2–3 minutes and pour it over the fish. Serve at once, garnished with the parsley.

Menu Suggestion
Serve with boiled new potatoes tossed in butter and chopped fresh mint, followed by Rhubarb and Orange Fool (page 111).

SPECIAL PARSLEY FISH PIE

| 1.00 | £ | 683 cals |

Serves 4

450 g (1 lb) haddock fillets

300 ml ($\frac{1}{2}$ pint) milk, plus 90 ml (6 tbsp)

1 bay leaf

6 peppercorns

1 onion, skinned and sliced

salt

65 g (2$\frac{1}{2}$ oz) butter or margarine

45 ml (3 tbsp) plain flour

freshly ground pepper

2 eggs, hard-boiled and chopped

150 ml (5 fl oz) single cream

30 ml (2 tbsp) chopped fresh parsley

100 g (4 oz) cooked prawns

900 g (2 lb) potatoes, peeled

1 egg, beaten, to glaze

1 Rinse and drain the fish. Place in a pan and pour over 300 ml ($\frac{1}{2}$ pint) of milk; add the bay leaf, peppercorns, onion and a pinch of salt. Bring to the boil and simmer for 10 minutes until just tender.

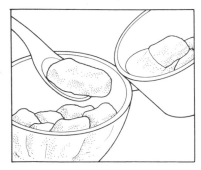

2 Lift from the pan, flake the flesh and remove the skin and bones. Strain the cooking liquid and reserve.

3 Make the sauce. Melt 40 g (1$\frac{1}{2}$ oz) of the butter in a pan, stir in the flour and cook gently for 1 minute, stirring. Remove the pan from the heat and gradually stir in the reserved cooking liquid. Bring to the boil, stirring, until sauce thickens, then cook for a further 2–3 minutes. Season to taste.

4 Add the eggs to the sauce with the fresh cream, fish, parsley and prawns. Check the seasoning, and spoon the mixture into a 1.1-litre (2-pint) pie dish.

5 Meanwhile, boil the potatoes, drain and mash without any liquid. Heat the remaining 90 ml (6 tbsp) of milk and remaining 25 g (1 oz) butter and beat into the potatoes; season.

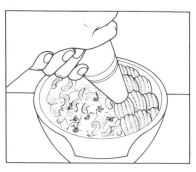

6 Spoon the potatoes into a piping bag and pipe across the fish mixture. Alternatively, spoon the potato over the fish and roughen the surface with a fork.

7 Bake in the oven at 200°C (400°F) mark 6 for 10–15 minutes, until the potato is set. Brush the beaten egg over the pie. Return to oven for a further 15 minutes, until golden brown.

Menu Suggestion

Serve with Deep-Fried Mushrooms with Herby Dressing (page 12), Peppered Carrots (page 98) and Poached Pears in Ginger Syrup (page 114).

ITALIAN FISH STEW

| 1.00 | 🥘 | £ £ | 481 cals |

Serves 4

good pinch of saffron strands

about 900 g (2 lb) mixed fish fillets (e.g. red mullet, bream, bass, brill, monkfish, plaice or cod)

10–12 whole prawns, cooked

60 ml (4 tbsp) olive oil

1 large onion, skinned and finely chopped

3 garlic cloves, skinned and crushed

2 slices of drained canned pimiento, sliced

450 g (1 lb) tomatoes, skinned, seeded and chopped

2 canned anchovy fillets, drained

150 ml ($\frac{1}{4}$ pint) dry white wine

150 ml ($\frac{1}{4}$ pint) water

2 bay leaves

45 ml (3 tbsp) chopped fresh basil

salt and freshly ground pepper

10–12 mussels, in their shells

4 slices of hot toast, to serve

1 Prepare the saffron water. Soak the saffron strands in a little boiling water for 30 minutes.

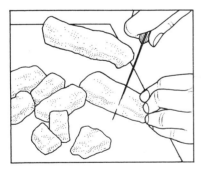

2 Meanwhile, skin the fish and cut into chunky bite-sized pieces. Shell the prawns.

3 Heat the oil in a large heavy-based pan, add the onion, garlic and pimiento and fry gently for 5 minutes until soft.

4 Add the tomatoes and anchovies and stir with a wooden spoon to break them up. Pour in the wine and the water and bring to the boil, then lower the heat and add the bay leaves and half the basil. Simmer uncovered for 20 minutes, stirring occasionally.

5 Add the firm fish to the tomato mixture, then strain in the saffron water and add salt and pepper to taste. Cook for 10 minutes, then add the delicate-textured fish and cook for a further 5 minutes or until tender.

6 Add the prawns and mussels and cook, covered, for 5 minutes or until the mussels open. Remove the bay leaves and discard.

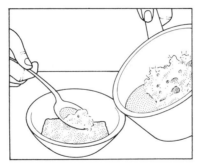

7 To serve, put one slice of toast in each of four individual soup bowls. Spoon over the soup, sprinkle with the remaining basil and serve at once.

Menu Suggestion
Serve with fresh French bread and a tossed green salad.

ITALIAN FISH STEW

This type of fish stew is popular in coastal regions, especially in the regions around the Adriatic Sea and in the southern part of Italy around Sicily.

There are numerous different versions of fish stew or soup, called *zuppa di pesce* in Italian, with recipes varying from one village and one cook to another—there are no hard and fast rules. *Burrida* is the famous fish and tomato stew from Genoa; it contains many unusual fish which are not available outside local waters, but it can be made successfully outside the region with monkfish, octopus and squid, together with clams, mussels and shrimps.

Around the Adriatic Sea, fish soup is called *brodetto*—the ones from Venice, Rimini and Ravenna being the most famous. These fish soups use similar fish to the Genoese *burrida*, but they do not contain tomatoes and they are traditionally served with bread fried or baked in oil—called *casada*. Another well-known Italian fish soup is *caciuccio Livornese*, a main course dish flavoured strongly with tomatoes and hot red peppers, and served with *casada*.

Don't worry if you can't find the authentic fish when making an Italian fish stew or soup. The recipe on this page suggests substitutes which are readily available outside Italy and which will taste equally good—as long as you use a good variety and make sure they are as fresh as possible. Try to include at least some red or grey mullet; monkfish is also a good buy—it has a strong flavour and dense texture, and does not break up easily during cooking.

Eggs and Cheese

For economical and nutritious meals, cheese and eggs are a must—and they're always to hand in the refrigerator to rustle up a meal at the last minute.

This chapter illustrates the versatility of cheese and eggs. Don't just confine them to toasted snacks—with a little imagination and ingenuity and the addition of herbs and spices they make interesting and unusual starters and main courses too.

SORREL SOUFFLÉ

1.00		481 cals

Serves 4

100 g (4 oz) sorrel

50 g (2 oz) butter or margarine

225 g (8 oz) button mushrooms, finely chopped

1 garlic clove, skinned and crushed

45 ml (3 tbsp) plain flour

200 ml (7 fl oz) milk

salt and freshly ground pepper

225 g (8 oz) Fontina or Gruyère cheese, rinded and grated

3 eggs, separated

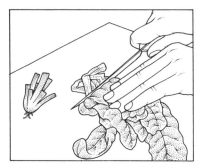

1 Trim any tough stalks off the sorrel; wash and drain the leaves then finely chop.

2 Melt the butter in a large saucepan, add the sorrel, mushrooms and crushed garlic. Stir over a high heat for 1–2 minutes. Stir in the flour and cook for a further 1 minute.

3 Remove from the heat and gradually stir in the milk and seasoning. Bring to the boil, stirring, then cook for 1 minute.

4 Remove from the heat and beat in 200 g (7 oz) cheese followed by the egg yolks.

5 Whisk the egg whites until stiff but not dry. Fold lightly into the sauce mixture. Spoon into a 1.4-litre (2½-pint) greased soufflé dish and sprinkle over remaining grated cheese to coat evenly.

6 Bake in the oven at 190°C (375°F) mark 5 for about 40 minutes or until well risen, browned and just set. Serve at once, piping hot.

Menu Suggestion

Serve as a light lunch dish with a fresh tomato and onion salad and buttered new potatoes.

SORREL SOUFFLÉ

The herb sorrel looks like spinach, but it has a rather stronger, more bitter flavour. The small quantity used here, when combined with white sauce, cheese and mushrooms, is quite delicious, but if you prefer a milder flavour you can use half spinach and half sorrel. Sorrel is not always easy to obtain in shops, but it is easy to grow in a sunny spot in the garden if you are fond of its unusual flavour—you will find it useful in summer to add interest to green salads. If you find sorrel difficult to obtain, you can of course make the soufflé with spinach instead.

Fontina is a unique Italian cheese from the mountainous Val D'Aosta region of north-west Italy. It is a semi-hard cheese with a sweet, nutty flavour and creamy texture. It makes an unusual addition to a cheeseboard, but it is most frequently used in cooking in Italy because of its excellent melting qualities—it is the traditional cheese to use in the Italian cheese fondue called *fonduta*. Look for it in Italian delicatessens, or use Swiss Gruyère or Emmental instead, they have similar flavours and melting qualities to Fontina, and are easier to obtain.

FETA CHEESE PUFFS WITH BASIL

| 0.25 | £ | ✳* | 274 cals |

* freeze after stage 4

Makes 8

225 g (8 oz) Feta cheese, grated

142 g (5 oz) natural yogurt

30 ml (2 tbsp) chopped fresh basil
   or 5 ml (1 tsp) dried

freshly ground pepper

397-g (14-oz) packet frozen puff
   pastry, thawed

beaten egg

fresh basil leaves, to garnish

1 Mix the grated cheese with the
   yogurt, basil and pepper.
(Don't add salt as the cheese adds
sufficient.)

2 Roll out the pastry *thinly* and
   cut out sixteen 10-cm (4-inch)
rounds. Fold and reroll the pastry
as necessary.

3 Place half the rounds on two
   baking sheets. Spoon the
cheese mixture into the centre of
each one.

4 Brush the pastry edges with
   egg. Cover with remaining
rounds, knocking up and pressing
the pastry edges together to seal.
Make a small slit in the top of each
pastry puff.

5 Glaze with beaten egg. Bake in
   the oven at 220°C (425°F)
mark 7 for about 15 minutes or
until well browned and crisp.
Serve warm, garnished with fresh
basil leaves.

Menu Suggestion
Serve as a starter with Afelia
(page 30) and Geranium Grape
Sorbet (page 115).

FETA CHEESE
Greek Feta cheese can be made
from either sheep's or goat's milk.
Vacuum packs, which tend to be
rather salty, are available at some
large supermarkets and good
delicatessens, but the best Feta
(sold loose in brine) is found in
Greek and Middle Eastern stores.

BLUE CHEESE CROQUETTES

| 1.00* | 🍳 | ✳* | 416–623 cals |

* plus 2–3 hours chilling; freeze after
stage 5

Serves 4–6

100 g (4 oz) celery

75 g (3 oz) butter or margarine

75 g (3 oz) plain flour, plus a little
   extra for coating

225 ml (8 fl oz) milk

175 g (6 oz) Blue Stilton cheese,
   grated

30 ml (2 tbsp) snipped fresh chives
   or 15 ml (1 tbsp) dried

2 eggs

freshly ground pepper

65 g (2½ oz) dried white
   breadcrumbs

vegetable oil, for deep frying

1 Finely chop the celery; sauté
   in the butter or margarine for
5–10 minutes until beginning to
become brown.

2 Stir in the flour; cook for 1
   minute. Off the heat stir in the
milk. Bring to the boil, stirring,
then cook for 1 minute—the mixture will be *very* thick.

3 Remove from the heat and stir
   in the grated cheese, chives,
one egg and pepper (the cheese
will add sufficient salt).

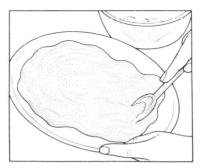

4 Spread the mixture out in a
   shallow dish, cover with damp
greaseproof paper and cool for 30
minutes. Refrigerate for 2–3 hours
to firm up.

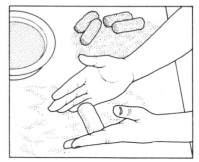

5 Shape the mixture into twelve
   croquettes then coat lightly in
flour, beaten egg and breadcrumbs.

6 Deep fry the croquettes at
   180°C (350°F), a few at a time,
for 3–4 minutes until golden
brown. Serve hot.

Menu Suggestion
Serve as a starter with Pork
Escalopes with Sage (page 42) and
Spiced Dried Fruit Compote
(page 116).

LOVAGE AND BLUE CHEESE OMELETTE

| 0.15 | £ | 430 cals |

Serves 2

4 eggs
10 ml (2 tsp) chopped fresh lovage
30 ml (2 tbsp) water
salt and freshly ground pepper
75 g (3 oz) Blue Cheshire cheese
15 g (½ oz) butter or margarine
lovage leaves, to garnish

1 Whisk together the eggs, lovage, water and seasoning. Coarsely grate the cheese, or cut it into thin slivers and set aside.

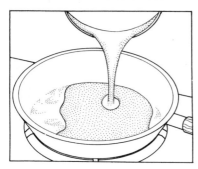

2 Heat the butter in a 20.5-cm (8-inch) non-stick frying pan. When foaming, pour in the egg mixture all at once.

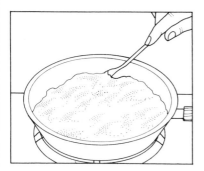

3 Cook over a moderate-high heat for a few minutes, drawing a fork through the omelette to allow the unset egg mixture to run through to the edges.

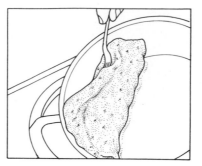

4 When set underneath but still creamy on top, scatter the cheese over the surface of the omelette. Leave for a few moments until the cheese starts to melt, then fold over the omelette into three.

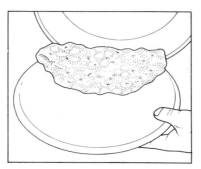

5 To serve, slide the omelette on to a serving plate. Garnish with lovage leaves. Divide in two for serving.

Menu Suggestion
Serve as a light lunch dish with new potatoes tossed in melted butter, sea salt and freshly ground black pepper.

BLUE CHEESE
There are numerous different blue cheeses on the market, some soft and creamy, others hard and crumbly. For this recipe a crumbly blue cheese is specified because this will have the correct melting qualities necessary for a quick-cooking omelette. French and Italian blue cheeses tend to be the soft and creamy type; British hard and semi-hard cheeses are the most suitable for omelette making. Choose from the following:

Blue Stilton is rich and strongly flavoured, a semi-hard cheese with a smooth texture. Young Stilton has a sharper flavour than the mellow matured cheese—to tell the age of a Stilton, check the colour of the cheese just below the rind. If the cheese is mature, it will be darker than in the centre.

Blue Cheshire is another semi-hard cheese, with a rich and robust flavour. The paste of this cheese is orange in colour, which gives a good contrast with the blue of the veining. It is a good melting cheese, and its flavour is pleasantly tangy.

Other British blue cheeses which are not so readily available but worth looking for at specialist cheese shops and delicatessens are *Blue Wensleydale* (a white cheese with delicate web-like blue veining) and *Blue Shropshire* (a dark yellow cheese with branching blue veins).

EGG MOUSSE

0.45* ☐ £ 189 cals

* plus 2 hours setting

Serves 10

1 small cucumber

salt

4 hard-boiled eggs, shelled and
  finely chopped

1 bunch of spring onions, washed,
  trimmed and finely chopped

150 ml ($\frac{1}{4}$ pint) thick mayonnaise

142 ml (5 fl oz) soured cream

finely grated rind of 1 lemon

22.5 ml ($1\frac{1}{2}$ tbsp) chopped fresh dill

freshly ground pepper

15 ml (3 tsp) gelatine

60 ml (4 tbsp) lemon juice

2 egg whites

fresh dill, cucumber and hard-
  boiled egg slices, to garnish

3 Meanwhile, put the eggs in a bowl with the spring onions, mayonnaise, soured cream, lemon rind, dill and salt and pepper to taste. Mix well.

4 In a separate heatproof bowl, sprinkle the gelatine over the lemon juice. Leave to soak for 5 minutes until spongy, then stand the bowl over a saucepan of hot water and heat gently until dissolved. Remove from the heat and leave to cool slightly.

5 Pat the cucumber with absorbent kitchen paper. Fold gently into the egg mixture with the dissolved gelatine until evenly mixed.

6 Whisk the egg whites until stiff, then fold into the mousse with a large metal spoon. Turn the mixture into a serving bowl or 1.4-litre ($2\frac{1}{2}$-pint) soufflé dish and level the surface. Chill in the refrigerator for 2 hours before serving garnished with dill sprigs, cucumber and hard-boiled egg slices.

Menu Suggestion

Serve as a starter with Porc au Poivre (page 35) and Poached Pears in Ginger Syrup (page 114).

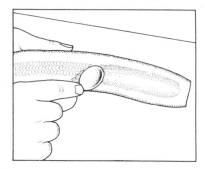

1 Peel the cucumber, cut in half lengthways, then scoop out and discard the seeds.

2 Chop cucumber flesh finely, place in a colander and sprinkle with salt. Cover with a plate, with weights on top; leave for 30 minutes until moisture is removed.

Spiced Pepper and Onion Flan

| 1.25 | 530 cals |

Serves 4

75 g (3 oz) block margarine

175 g (6 oz) plain flour, plus 30 ml (2 tbsp)

salt

15 ml (1 tbsp) vegetable oil

2 onions, skinned and thinly sliced

1 red pepper, seeded and sliced

25 g (1 oz) butter

5 ml (1 tsp) ground cumin

150 ml ($\frac{1}{4}$ pint) milk

142 g (5 oz) natural yogurt

2 egg yolks

30 ml (2 tbsp) grated Parmesan

1 Make the pastry. Rub the margarine into 175 g (6 oz) flour with a pinch of salt. Bind to a manageable dough with cold water. Knead until smooth.

2 Roll out the dough on a lightly floured surface and use to line a 20.5-cm (8-inch) plain flan ring placed on a baking sheet.

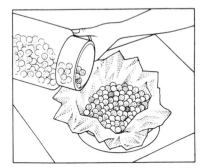

3 Chill for 15–20 minutes, then line with foil and baking beans. Bake blind in the oven at 200°C (400°F) mark 6 for 10–15 minutes until set but not browned.

4 Heat the oil in a frying pan. Sauté the sliced onions and pepper, reserving a few slices to garnish, in the hot oil for 4–5 minutes. Put into the flan case.

5 Melt the butter, stir in 30 ml (2 tbsp) flour and cumin. Cook for 2 minutes before adding the milk and yogurt. Bring to the boil, stirring briskly, simmer for 2–3 minutes. Beat in the egg yolks.

6 Pour over the onion and pepper and sprinkle with Parmesan. Cook in the oven at 190°C (375°F) mark 5 for 35–40 minutes. Serve hot garnished with pepper slices.

Menu Suggestion

Serve as a lunch or supper dish with a green salad tossed in a sharp vinaigrette dressing.

HERBY BRIE QUICHE

| 1.25 | £ £ ✳ | 473–709 cals |

Serves 4–6

150 g (5 oz) plain flour

5 ml (1 tsp) dried mixed herbs

salt

50 g (2 oz) butter

25 g (1 oz) lard

1 egg yolk

a little beaten egg white

225 g (8 oz) ripe Brie

150 ml (5 fl oz) double cream

3 eggs, lightly beaten

30 ml (2 tbsp) chopped fresh mixed
herbs (e.g. thyme, marjoram,
parsley, chives)

freshly ground pepper

1 Make the pastry. Sift the flour into a bowl with the herbs and a pinch of salt. Add the butter and lard in small pieces and cut into the flour with a knife.

2 Rub the fat into the flour until the mixture resembles fine breadcrumbs, then stir in the egg yolk. Gather the mixture into a ball of dough, then knead lightly until smooth.

3 Roll out on a floured surface. Use to line a 20-cm (8-inch) plain flan ring set on a baking sheet. Refrigerate for 20 minutes.

4 Prick the base of the dough lightly with a fork, then line with foil and weight down with baking beans. Bake blind in the oven at 200°C (400°F) mark 6 for 10 minutes.

5 Remove the foil and the beans, brush the inside of the pastry case with the beaten egg white, then return to the oven and bake for a further 5 minutes.

6 Remove the rind from the cheese, cut into squares and place in the base of the pastry case. Soften the cheese with a fork and gradually work in the cream to make a smooth mixture. Whisk in the beaten eggs, then the herbs and salt and pepper to taste.

7 Pour the filling into the pastry case. Bake in the oven at 180°C (350°F) mark 4 for 30 minutes until the filling is just set and the rind from the cheese has formed a golden crust on top. Leave to stand at room temperature for 15 minutes before serving.

Menu Suggestion
Serve as a lunch or supper dish with Hot Beetroot with Horseradish Sauce (page 101) and fresh French bread.

BRIE CHEESE
This soft, creamy cheese originated in the province of La Brie in Ile de France, but is now made in factories in other countries besides France— Germany and Denmark, for example, have thriving Brie industries.

Brie is much esteemed by the French, who have called it *roi de fromages*—'the king of cheeses'— since the year 1815 when it was the winner of an international cheese competition in Vienna. Genuine French Bries often bear the name of their exact place of origin, but this practice is dying out and most simply state the country where they were made. When buying fresh Brie cheese, it is best to buy it freshly cut from a large flat round or wheel at a specialist cheese shop or delicatessen—this is the only way to ensure the cheese is in perfect condition. A ripened cow's milk cheese, a perfect Brie should have a soft, downy rind and a creamy, supple paste. Avoid cheese which has a hard rind or which is either strong-smelling and runny in the centre, or which has a chalky line running through it.

Ripe Brie does not keep well and should be used on the day of purchase. If you need to store it for a few hours, wrap it loosely in foil and place in the least cold part of the refrigerator. Allow to come to room temperature (unwrapped) for 1 hour before required.

Vegetables

Vegetable dishes should not be overlooked when planning a menu — everyone appreciates crisp and crunchy fresh vegetables to accompany their main course, whatever it may be. The addition of freshly chopped herbs or subtle spices — tossed in melted butter with freshly ground sea salt and black pepper — can transform even the plainest of vegetable dishes; the recipes in this chapter will give you plenty more ideas.

HOT POTATOES WITH DILL

| 0.35 | £ | 174 cals |

Serves 6

900 g (2 lb) potatoes

salt

4 spring onions, washed and finely chopped

15 ml (1 tbsp) chopped fresh dill and a sprig, to garnish

freshly ground pepper

142 ml (5 fl oz) soured cream

1 Place the potatoes in cold, salted water, bring to the boil and cook for 12–15 minutes until tender.

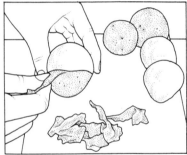

2 Drain the potatoes, leave until just cool enough to handle, then remove the skins.

3 Cut the potatoes into small dice and place in a bowl. Add the chopped onions to the potatoes with the dill and salt and pepper to taste.

4 Thin the soured cream, if necessary, with a little boiling water or milk, stir it into the potatoes and toss gently.

5 Leave to stand for a few minutes so that the flavours can blend. To serve, garnish with a sprig of dill.

CHINESE VEGETABLE STIR-FRY

| 0.15 | £ | 157 cals |

Serves 4

1 turnip, peeled

4 small carrots, peeled

4 celery sticks

2 young leeks, washed and trimmed

30 ml (2 tbsp) sesame oil

15 ml (1 tbsp) vegetable oil

100 g (4 oz) beansprouts, washed and drained

10 ml (2 tsp) soy sauce

5 ml (1 tsp) white wine vinegar

5 ml (1 tsp) soft brown sugar

5 ml (1 tsp) five-spice powder

salt

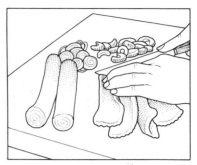

2 Slice the celery and leeks finely. Then heat the oils in a wok, and add the prepared vegetables with the beansprouts. Stir-fry over moderate heat for 3–4 minutes, then sprinkle in the soy sauce, wine vinegar, sugar, five-spice powder and salt to taste. Stir-fry for 1 further minute. Serve at once, while piping hot.

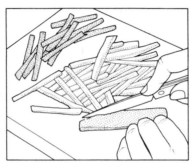

1 Using a sharp knife, cut the turnip and the peeled carrots into matchstick strips.

STIR-FRYING

The beauty of the Chinese stir-frying technique is that it is so quick and easy—perfect for entertaining when you want to be with your guests as much as possible. With stir-frying, everything can be prepared ahead of time so that all you have to do is quickly cook the ingredients at the last moment.

A Chinese wok is best for stir-frying, but not absolutely essential. The reason why a wok is so successful is that the bottom is round and cone-shaped so that the heat is concentrated in the centre—food cooks very fast when it is pushed to the base of the pan. A Chinese wok keeps an intense level of heat through-out cooking, but if you don't have one, a cast iron frying-pan can be used instead.

Traditionally, very long chop-sticks are used to push the food around the wok during stir fry-ing, but if you find it easier you can use a wooden spatula or fork.

SAG ALOO *(CURRIED SPINACH AND POTATOES)*

| 0.35 | £ | ✳ | 190–285 cals |

Serves 4–6

two 225-g (8-oz) packets frozen leaf spinach, thawed and drained

50 g (2 oz) ghee or vegetable oil

1 onion, skinned and thinly sliced

2 garlic cloves, skinned and crushed

10 ml (2 tsp) ground coriander

5 ml (1 tsp) mustard seeds

2.5 ml ($\frac{1}{2}$ tsp) ground turmeric

1.25–2.5 ml ($\frac{1}{4}$–$\frac{1}{2}$ tsp) chilli powder, according to taste

salt

450 g (1 lb) potatoes, peeled and cut roughly into cubes

150 ml ($\frac{1}{4}$ pint) water

1 Put the spinach in a heavy-based pan and place over very gentle heat for about 5 minutes to drive off as much liquid as possible.

2 Meanwhile, melt the ghee in a separate heavy-based pan. Add the onion, garlic, spices and salt to taste and fry gently for about 5 minutes, stirring frequently.

3 Add the potatoes and fold gently into the spice mixture, then pour in the water. Bring to the boil, then lower the heat and simmer, uncovered, for 10 minutes. Stir occasionally during this time and add a few more spoonfuls of water if necessary.

4 Fold the spinach gently in to the potato mixture. Simmer for a further 5–10 minutes until the potatoes are just tender. To serve, taste and adjust seasoning, then turn into a warmed serving dish. Serve hot.

SAG ALOO

This Indian vegetable accompaniment (*sag* meaning spinach and *aloo* potatoes) would go particularly well with the Madras Beef Curry on page 38. As an alternative to spinach you could use cauliflower florets to make *Aloo Gobi*: blanch **450 g (1 lb) cauliflower florets** in **boiling salted water** in stage 1, then add to the curried potatoes in stage 4.

VEGETABLE PILAU

| 0.45 | £ | 320 cals |

Serves 6

1 small cauliflower, washed

225 g (8 oz) leeks

50 g (2 oz) butter or margarine

450 g (1 lb) carrots, peeled and thinly sliced

350 g (12 oz) long grain rice

5 ml (1 tsp) ground cardamom

5 ml (1 tsp) paprika

2.5 ml ($\frac{1}{2}$ tsp) ground cloves

2.5 ml ($\frac{1}{2}$ tsp) ground cinnamon

1 litre (1$\frac{3}{4}$ pints) chicken stock

salt and freshly ground pepper

1 fresh green pepper

lime twist, to garnish

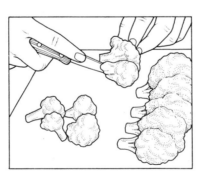

1 With a sharp knife, divide the cauliflower into small florets, discarding any coarse, thick stems.

2 Cut the leeks crosswise into 1-cm ($\frac{1}{2}$-inch) slices, discarding any coarse leaves; wash and drain.

3 Heat the butter in a large flameproof casserole. Fry the sliced carrots, cauliflower and leeks for 5 minutes until lightly coloured.

4 Stir in rice with cardamom, paprika, cloves and cinnamon and cook for 1 minute, stirring.

5 Pour in stock, season well, bring to boil. Cover and cook in the oven at 180°C (350°F) mark 4 for 15 minutes.

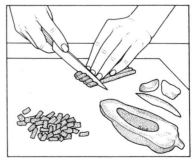

6 Halve, seed and dice the pepper and stir into the pilau. Return covered casserole to the oven for a further 10 minutes. Garnish with a twist of lime.

CABBAGE WITH CARAWAY

| 0.15 | 110 cals |

Serves 6

1.4 kg (3 lb) green cabbage
salt
50 g (2 oz) butter or margarine
5 ml (1 tsp) caraway seeds
freshly ground pepper

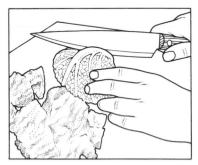

1 Shred the cabbage finely, discarding any core or tough outer leaves. Wash well under cold running water.

2 Cook in a large pan of boiling salted water for 2 minutes only—the cabbage should retain its crispness and texture. Drain well.

3 Melt the butter in the saucepan; add the drained cabbage with the caraway seeds and seasoning. Stir over a moderate heat for 2–3 minutes until the cabbage is really hot. Adjust seasoning and serve immediately.

PEPPERED CARROTS

0.20	157 cals

Serves 4

50 g (2 oz) butter or margarine

5 ml (1 tsp) sugar

450 g (1 lb) carrots, peeled or scrubbed and thinly sliced

3 spring onions, washed and trimmed

1.25 ml ($\frac{1}{4}$ tsp) cayenne pepper or to taste

45 ml (3 tbsp) soured cream

salt and freshly ground pepper

1 Melt the butter with the sugar in a deep sauté pan which has a tightly fitting lid. Put the carrots into the pan, cover tightly and cook gently for 10–15 minutes until tender.

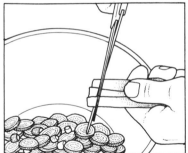

2 Remove the lid from the pan and snip in the spring onions with a pair of sharp kitchen scissors. Transfer carrots and onions with a slotted spoon to a serving dish and keep warm.

3 Stir the cayenne pepper and soured cream into the pan. Taste and adjust seasoning, and warm through for 1–2 minutes. Pour over the carrots and serve.

TURNIPS IN CURRY CREAM SAUCE

0.30	270 cals

Serves 4

700 g (1½ lb) small turnips

salt

50 g (2 oz) butter or margarine

1 onion, skinned and finely chopped

100 g (4 oz) cooking apple

50 g (2 oz) sultanas

5 ml (1 tsp) mild curry powder

5 ml (1 tsp) plain flour

150 ml (¼ pint) dry cider

150 ml (5 fl oz) single cream

10 ml (2 tsp) lemon juice

freshly ground pepper

1 Peel the turnips, boil in salted water for 10–15 minutes until just tender. Meanwhile, make the sauce. Melt the butter, add the onion, cover and cook gently for 10 minutes until soft and tinged with colour. Peel and finely chop the apple and add to the onion, together with the sultanas, curry powder and flour. Cook, stirring constantly, for 3–4 minutes.

2 Pour the cider into the pan, bring to the boil, bubble gently for 2 minutes, stirring. Off the heat stir in the cream, lemon juice and seasoning. Keep warm without boiling.

3 Drain the turnips in a colander. To serve, place in a heated dish and pour over the curry cream sauce. Serve immediately.

HOT BEETROOT WITH HORSERADISH

| 0.20 | f | 53–80 cals |

Serves 4–6

450 g (1 lb) cooked beetroot

15 ml (1 tbsp) caster sugar

60 ml (4 tbsp) red wine vinegar

30 ml (2 tbsp) freshly grated horseradish

salt and freshly ground pepper

15 ml (1 tbsp) cornflour

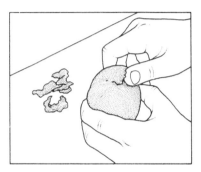

1 Rub the skin off the beetroot carefully, using your fingers. Slice the beetroot neatly into rounds.

2 Put the beetroot in a large heavy-based pan, then sprinkle with the sugar. Pour in the wine vinegar and add the horseradish with salt and pepper to taste.

3 Bring to the boil, without stirring, then lower the heat, cover and simmer gently for 10 minutes.

4 Transfer the beetroot slices carefully with a slotted spoon to a warmed serving dish. Mix the cornflour to a paste with a little cold water, then stir into the cooking liquid in the pan. Boil for 1–2 minutes, stirring vigorously until the liquid thickens. To serve, taste and adjust seasoning, then pour over the beetroot. Serve immediately.

SPICY VEGETABLE PIE

1.00* 🔲 £ ✳ 690 cals

* plus 2½ hours cooling and chilling

Serves 4

4 carrots, peeled and thinly sliced

4 leeks, washed, trimmed and
    thickly sliced

6 courgettes, washed, trimmed and
    thinly sliced

salt

175 g (6 oz) butter or margarine

1 onion, skinned and sliced

10 ml (2 tsp) ground cumin

175 g (6 oz) wholemeal flour

450 ml (¾ pint) milk plus 30 ml
    (2 tbsp)

100 g (4 oz) Cheddar cheese, grated

1.25 ml (¼ tsp) ground mace

freshly ground pepper

45 ml (3 tbsp) chopped fresh
    coriander or parsley

2.5 ml (½ tsp) baking powder

beaten egg, to glaze

10 ml (2 tsp) grated Parmesan

pinch of cayenne or paprika

1 Make the vegetable filling.
Blanch the carrots, leeks and
courgettes in boiling salted water
for 1 minute only. Drain well.

2 Melt 40 g (1½ oz) butter in a
heavy-based pan, add the
onion and cumin and fry gently
for 5 minutes until soft. Add the
carrots, leeks and courgettes and
fry for a further 5 minutes, stirring
to coat in the onion mixture. Remove from the heat and set aside.

3 Melt 65 g (2½ oz) butter in a
separate pan, sprinkle in 50 g
(2 oz) of the flour and cook for
1–2 minutes, stirring, until lightly
coloured. Remove from the heat
and whisk in 450 ml (¾ pint) milk;
return to the heat and simmer for
5 minutes until thick and smooth.

4 Stir in the Cheddar cheese,
mace and salt and pepper to
taste. Fold into the vegetables with
the chopped coriander and 30 ml
(2 tbsp) milk then turn into a 900-
ml (1½-pint) ovenproof pie dish.
Leave for 2 hours until cold.

5 Make the pastry. Sift 100 g
(4 oz) flour, baking powder
and a pinch of salt into a bowl.
Rub in 50 g (2 oz) butter until the
mixture resembles fine breadcrumbs, then add just enough
water to mix to a firm dough.

6 Gather the dough into a ball,
knead lightly and wrap in
cling film; chill for 30 minutes.

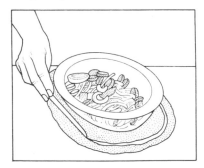

7 Remove the dough from the
refrigerator and roll out on a
floured surface. Cut out a thin
strip long enough to go around the
rim of the pie dish. Moisten rim
with water; place strip on rim.

8 Roll out the remaining dough
for a lid, moisten the strip of
dough, then place the lid on top
and press to seal. Knock up and
flute edge. Decorate the top.

9 Brush pastry with beaten egg;
dust with Parmesan and
cayenne. Bake in the oven at 190°C
(375°F) mark 5 for 20–25 minutes.

Menu Suggestion
Serve as a main dish to follow
Deep-fried Mushrooms with
Herby Dressing (page 12) and
Lemon Balm Syllabub (page 105).

Desserts and Puddings

Don't confine your herbs, spices and flavourings to savoury dishes—in this chapter you will see lots of ways they can be used in sweet dishes too.
Lemon balm, orange flower water and mint add flavour to fresh fruit, while nutmeg and cloves work spicy wonders for bland milk puds— welcome in winter when jaded palates need revival!

LEMON BALM SYLLABUB

| 0.10* | £ £ | 342–456 cals |

* plus 2–3 hours chilling

Serves 6–8

30 ml (2 tbsp) finely chopped lemon balm leaves

600 ml (1 pint) double cream

150 ml (¼ pint) sweet white wine

grated rind and juice of 2 lemons

5 ml (1 tsp) caster sugar, or to taste

nutmeg, lemon shreds and sprigs of lemon balm, to decorate

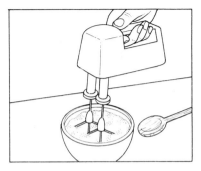

1 Whisk together all the ingredients except the nutmeg, lemon shreds and lemon balm, until they reach the consistency of custard.

2 Leave in the refrigerator for 2–3 hours to chill. To serve, spoon into tall glasses, grate a little nutmeg on the top and garnish with lemon shreds and sprigs of lemon balm.

Menu Suggestion
Serve with Mussels with Garlic and Parsley (page 23) and Duck with Spiced Stuffing (page 47).

SUMMER FRUIT SALAD

1.20*	£ £	117–176 cals

* plus 30 minutes cooling

Serves 4–6

100 g (4 oz) sugar

200 ml (7 fl oz) water

few fresh mint sprigs

1 strip of orange peel

225 g (8 oz) fresh strawberries

225 g (8 oz) fresh raspberries

1 small Ogen melon

30 ml (2 tbsp) orange-flavoured liqueur

30 ml (2 tbsp) finely chopped fresh mint

few whole fresh mint leaves, to decorate

1 Put the sugar in a heavy-based pan, add the water and heat gently for 5–10 minutes until the sugar has dissolved, stirring occasionally.

2 Add the mint sprigs and orange peel, then boil the syrup rapidly for 5 minutes, without stirring. Remove from the heat and leave for about 1 hour until completely cold.

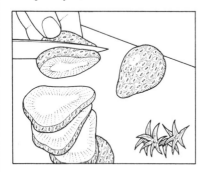

3 Meanwhile, prepare the fruit. Hull the strawberries, then slice them lengthways.

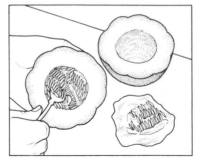

4 Leave the raspberries whole. Cut the melon in half, scoop out and discard the seeds.

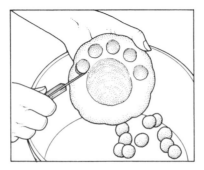

5 Cut the flesh into balls using a melon baller. Remove the mint sprigs and orange peel from the cold syrup, then stir in the liqueur and chopped mint.

6 Put the fruit in a serving bowl, pour over the syrup, then carefully fold together. Chill in the refrigerator for at least 30 minutes. Serve chilled, decorated with whole fresh mint leaves.

Menu Suggestion

Serve with Iced Sorrel Soup (page 11) and Turkey in Spiced Yogurt (page 52).

MELONS

The Ogen melon specified in this Summer Fruit Salad is available most of the year from specialist greengrocers and markets. The name 'Ogen' comes from the kibbutz in Israel where these melons were first grown.

Ogen melons are well worth looking for, because their flesh is very sweet—perfect for summer fruit salads, and also for winter desserts when other fresh fruits are scarce. Ogen melons are easily identified by their yellowy-green, stripy skins and their almost perfect round shape. Most Ogen melons are small enough for 1 serving, but large ones are also available which will serve 2–3 people. Both sizes are ideal for making into melon baskets—a pretty way to serve a fruit salad such as the one on this page. If you buy small Ogens, make individual baskets for each place setting; large Ogens, like honeydew melons, make spectacular table centrepieces.

To make a melon basket

1 Level the base of the melon so that it will stand upright.
2 With the tip of a sharp knife, score horizontally around the centre of the melon, keeping the line as straight as possible.
3 Cut down from the top of the melon to the scored line, working about 1 cm ($\frac{1}{2}$ inch) to one side of the centre.
4 Cut through the scored line on one side so that a wedge-shaped piece of melon is removed.
5 Repeat steps 3 and 4 so that both sides are removed.
6 Carefully scrape away the melon flesh inside the 'handle' left in the centre.
7 Scoop out and discard the seeds, then remove the flesh in the bottom half of the basket with a melon baller or sharp knife. Combine with the cut flesh from the reserved wedges.

SWEET INDIAN SAFFRON RICE

| 1.20 | 🍴 £ | 411–617 cals |

Serves 4–6

10–12 large strands of saffron

600 ml (1 pint) cold water, plus 30 ml (2 tbsp) boiling water

225 g (8 oz) basmati rice

75 g (3 oz) sugar

pinch of freshly grated nutmeg

30 ml (2 tbsp) ghee or vegetable oil

seeds from 6 green cardamom pods, crushed

4 cloves

2.5-cm (1-inch) stick of cinnamon

100 g (4 oz) blanched almonds, sliced or chopped

50 g (2 oz) unsalted pistachio nuts, sliced or chopped

25 g (1 oz) raisins

15 ml (1 tbsp) lemon juice

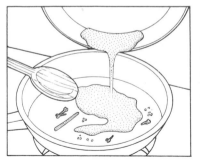

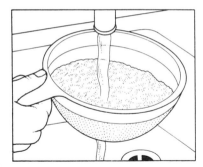

1 Let the saffron infuse in the boiling water for 30 minutes. Put the rice in a sieve and then wash thoroughly under a running cold tap until the water runs clear; soak it in cold water for 15 minutes.

2 Drain the rice and place in a heavy-based saucepan with 300 ml (½ pint) water. Strain in saffron water. Bring to boil, stir once, then cover with a tight-fitting lid. Reduce heat and cook for 12–15 minutes until water is absorbed and rice is parboiled.

3 In a separate pan, dissolve the sugar in the remaining water. Add the nutmeg and bring to the boil. Continue boiling for 2–3 minutes, then remove from heat.

4 Heat the ghee or butter in a large heavy-based pan, add the crushed cardamom seeds, cloves and the cinnamon. Stirring all the time, fry these for 2–3 minutes. Stand well back, in case of sputtering, and pour in the syrup. Bring to the boil, then reduce heat to low.

5 Add the parboiled rice, with the sliced or chopped almonds, pistachio nuts, raisins and the lemon juice. Stir just once, cover with a tight-fitting lid and cook for a further 10 minutes until the syrup is completely absorbed. The rice should be light and fluffy and a delicate yellow colour.

Menu Suggestion
Serve with Shamee Kebab with Yogurt Mint Dip (page 24) and Tandoori Chicken (page 51).

BASMATI RICE
Although ordinary long grain rice can be used to make this Indian dessert, basmati rice will give the dish authenticity. Basmati rice comes from the foothills of the Himalayas; it is expensive, but well worth using for all Indian dishes—sweet and savoury. Buy it loose by the kg (lb) in oriental grocers. Before using, basmati rice must be washed under cold running water until the water runs clear, then soaked in cold water for 15 minutes.

RHUBARB AND ORANGE FOOL

| 1.35* | £ ✳ | 201 cals |

*plus 1–2 hours chilling

Serves 6

450 g (1 lb) rhubarb

grated rind and juice of 1 orange

pinch of cinnamon

25–50 g (1–2 oz) sugar

300 ml (10 fl oz) whipping cream

5 ml (1 tsp) orange flower water

shredded orange rind, to decorate

sponge fingers, to serve

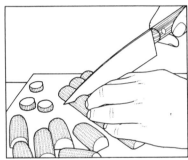

1 Wipe the rhubarb and chop into 2.5-cm (1-inch) pieces, discarding the leaves and the white ends of the stalks.

2 Put the rhubarb, orange rind, juice, cinnamon, and sugar into a pan and cook gently, covered, for about 15 minutes.

3 Remove the lid and boil rapidly for 10 minutes, stirring frequently, until the mixture becomes a thick purée. Cool for 1 hour.

4 When cool, whip the cream until stiff. Fold into the mixture with the orange flower water to taste. Spoon into glasses and chill for 1–2 hours until required. Decorate with orange rind and serve with sponge fingers.

Menu Suggestion
Serve with Deep-Fried Mushrooms with Herby Dressing (page 12) and Chicken with Saffron (page 56).

CHOCOLATE AND VANILLA ROULADE

| 1.45 | ⊟ £ ❋* | 306 cals |

* freeze after stage 2

Serves 6

100 g (4 oz) vanilla sugar (see page 152)

4 eggs

60 ml (4 tbsp) cocoa powder

2.5 ml (½ tsp) ground cinnamon

caster sugar

150 ml (5 fl oz) double cream

icing sugar and strawberries, to decorate

1 Line a 30 × 18 cm (12 × 7 inch) Swiss roll tin with greaseproof paper, grease and flour. In a bowl, beat the sugar and the eggs together until the mixture is thick and pale (see right). Sift and fold in the cocoa powder and cinnamon and pour into the prepared tin.

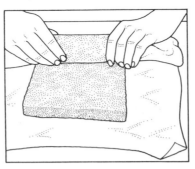

2 Bake in the oven at 200°C (400°F) mark 6 for 10–15 minutes then turn out on to a sheet of greaseproof paper coated with caster sugar. Cover with a sheet of greaseproof paper and roll with the paper inside. Leave to cool on a wire rack.

3 Whip the cream until it is just holding its shape. When the cake is cold, unroll and remove the paper. Spread with the whipped cream. Roll up, dredge with icing sugar and decorate with strawberries.

Menu Suggestion

Serve with Stuffed Tarragon Tomatoes (page 20) and Fricassée of Monkfish with Coriander (page 71).

MAKING A SWISS ROLL

The basis of this French *roulade* is a simple whisked sponge, i.e. a fatless sponge made by whisking together eggs and sugar until they are thick, pale and creamy, then folding in flour—or in this case, cocoa powder. The whisking stage is a very important one, to incorporate as much air as possible so that the finished texture of the cake is very delicate.

If you have a tabletop electric mixer, then the eggs and sugar can be whisked successfully in this. Alternatively, put the eggs and sugar in a heatproof bowl standing over a pan of gently simmering water and whisk with a balloon whisk or hand-held electric beater. When the mixture is thick enough to hold a ribbon trail, remove the bowl from the heat and continue whisking until cold before folding in the dry ingredients.

POACHED PEARS IN GINGER SYRUP

[1.00*] 🏺 ✳ [199 cals]

* plus 1–2 hours cooling and overnight chilling

Serves 4

150 ml (¼ pint) dry white wine

300 ml (½ pint) water

75 ml (5 tbsp) ginger wine

75 g (3 oz) soft brown sugar

1 strip lemon rind

1 cinnamon stick

4 firm pears

30 ml (2 tbsp) preserved ginger in syrup, thinly sliced

pouring cream, to serve

1 Pour the white wine into a large heavy-based pan. Add the water, the ginger wine, sugar, lemon rind and cinnamon. Heat gently until sugar has dissolved then remove from the heat.

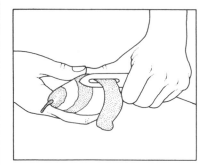

2 Using a vegetable peeler or cannelle knife, peel the pears from top to bottom in a spiral pattern. Leave the stalks on.

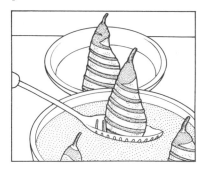

3 Put the pears in the wine and simmer gently for 30 minutes. Transfer to a serving bowl.

4 Boil the liquid in the pan until reduced by half, then strain and stir in the preserved ginger. Pour over the pears in the bowl.

5 Leave the pears for 1–2 hours until completely cold, then chill in the refrigerator overnight, spooning the syrup over them occasionally. Serve chilled, with pouring cream.

Menu Suggestion
Serve with Spicy Crab Dip (page 13) and Minted Lamb Grill (page 27).

TYPES OF PEAR
Pears are a difficult fruit to buy because they bruise easily and it seems almost impossible to get them at the correct degree of ripeness for eating. For cooking, however, firm pears are a little easier to come by. Both dessert and culinary varieties can be used, but some are more suitable than others. For this recipe, try to get firm Conference or slightly underripe Comice.

GERANIUM GRAPE SORBET

1.00* 🗇 ✳ 160 cals	

* plus 3–4 hours freezing

Serves 6

100 g (4 oz) sugar

300 ml (½ pint) water

15 ml (1 tbsp) chopped rose- or
  lemon-scented geranium leaves

700 g (1½ lb) seedless green grapes

90 ml (6 tbsp) dry white vermouth

2 egg whites

rose- or lemon-scented geranium
  leaves, to decorate

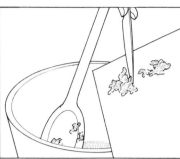

1 Make the sugar syrup. Dissolve the sugar in the water over a low heat. Bring to the boil and boil gently for 10 minutes. Add leaves, cover and cool.

2 Purée the grapes in a blender or food processor and then work through a sieve. There should be 600 ml (1 pint) purée. Add the vermouth and the strained sugar syrup, mix well, and pour this mixture into a container suitable for freezing (such as an ice-cube tray without divisions). Freeze for about 1 hour until half frozen and mushy.

3 Turn the half frozen mixture into a large bowl and break up with a fork.

4 Whisk the egg whites until stiff and fold into the grape mixture. Return to the container and freeze for about 2–3 hours until firm. Serve straight from the freezer, decorated with geranium leaves.

Menu Suggestion
Serve with Feta Cheese Puffs with Basil (page 84) and Chicken with Tarragon Sauce (page 54).

SPICED DRIED FRUIT COMPOTE

0.50*	£	218 cals

* plus 1–2 hours cooling and at least 2 hours chilling

Serves 4

15 ml (1 tbsp) jasmine tea

2.5 ml ($\frac{1}{2}$ tsp) ground cinnamon

1.25 ml ($\frac{1}{4}$ tsp) ground cloves

300 ml ($\frac{1}{2}$ pint) boiling water

100 g (4 oz) dried apricots, soaked overnight, drained

100 g (4 oz) dried prunes, soaked overnight, drained and stoned

100 g (4 oz) dried apple rings

150 ml ($\frac{1}{4}$ pint) dry white wine

50 g (2 oz) sugar

toasted flaked almonds, to decorate

1 Put tea, cinnamon and cloves in a bowl; pour in boiling water. Leave for 20 minutes.

2 Put dried fruit in a saucepan, then strain in tea and spice liquid. Add wine and sugar; heat gently until sugar has dissolved.

3 Simmer for 20 minutes until tender, then cover and leave for 1–2 hours until cold.

4 Turn the compote into a serving bowl and chill for at least 2 hours. Sprinkle with almonds just before serving.

Menu Suggestion
Serve with Mussels with Garlic and Parsley (page 23) and Sorrel Stuffed Lamb (page 35).

Baking

Cakes and other bakes take on a new dimension with spicy additions. From dark gooey ginger cakes and plain Victorian seed cakes to savoury doughs, warm and waiting to be split and buttered.

Baking is a satisfying art—and sweet spices make aromas wafting from your kitchen even more wonderful.

Dark Ginger Cake

1.45*	£	✳*	332–442 cals

* plus 2 hours cooling, freeze after stage 3

Serves 6–8

75 g (3 oz) black treacle

75 g (3 oz) golden syrup

50 g (2 oz) dark soft brown sugar

75 g (3 oz) butter or block margarine

225 g (8 oz) flour

10 ml (2 tsp) ground ginger

5 ml (1 tsp) mixed spice

5 ml (1 tsp) bicarbonate of soda

1 egg, beaten

100 ml (4 fl oz) milk

100 g (4 oz) icing sugar

15 ml (1 tbsp) warm water

50 g (2 oz) stem ginger, drained and sliced

1 Base-line and grease an 18-cm (7-inch) round deep cake tin. In a saucepan, gently heat the treacle, syrup, sugar and butter for 5 minutes until blended.

2 Sift the flour, spices and bi-carbonate of soda together into a bowl. Make a well in the centre and pour in the treacle mixture with egg and milk. Beat well with a wooden spoon until smooth.

3 Pour into the prepared tin and bake in the oven at 150°C (300°F) mark 2 for about 1 hour 30 minutes. Turn out on to a wire rack to cool for at least 2 hours.

4 To make the glacé icing, sift the icing sugar into a bowl and gradually add the water. The icing should be thick enough to coat the back of a spoon. If necessary add more water or sugar to adjust the consistency. Use at once to decorate the cake. Leave for 30 minutes to set slightly then decorate with the ginger.

GINGER

This spicy, iced version of old–fashioned gingerbread contains two different forms of ginger—ground ginger in the cake, stem ginger in the icing. Both come from the ginger root, a spice which has origins long before recorded history, when it was used as a medicine rather than a flavouring. Most of the ginger we buy comes from the Far East, where it first originated.

Ground ginger is made by grinding the dried root very finely. Jamaica ginger is said to be the finest and most delicate in flavour, but it is rare that the type of ginger is specified.

Stem ginger is also called pre-served or Chinese ginger. It is the young tender roots which are cleaned and peeled then sim-mered in a heavy syrup. Look for it in the prettily patterned Chinese jars, especially around Christmas time.

APRICOT CRUNCH

1.15* £ ✳ 195 cals

* plus 1½ hours cooling

Makes 16 wedges

75 g (3 oz) dried apricots

200 ml (⅓ pint) water

100 g (4 oz) butter

100 g (4 oz) demerara sugar

75 ml (5 tbsp) golden syrup

200 g (7 oz) crunchy toasted muesli cereal

140 g (5 oz) rolled oats

2.5 ml (½ tsp) mixed spice

10 ml (2 tsp) lemon juice

1 Base-line two 18-cm (7-inch) round sandwich tins with non-stick paper.

2 Simmer the apricots gently in the water for about 10 minutes, or until softened. Blend contents of pan to form a smooth purée. Cool for about 1 hour.

3 Slowly melt the butter, sugar and syrup. Stir in the cereal and oats and continue stirring until thoroughly combined. Add the puréed apricots, mixed spice and lemon juice. Mix well.

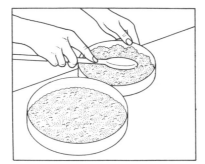

4 Divide the mixture between the prepared tins and spread evenly over the base. Press down well to level the surface.

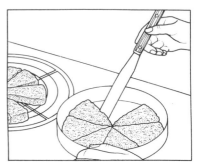

5 Bake in the oven at 180°C (350°F) mark 4 for about 35 minutes. Cut each round into eight wedges. Cool in the tin for 30 minutes until firm. Carefully ease the wedges out of the tin and store in an airtight container when completely cold.

LEMON SEED CAKE

| 1.35* | £ | ✳* | 604–806 cals |

* plus 1 hour cooling; freeze after stage 3

Serves 6–8

325 g (11 oz) butter

175 g (6 oz) soft brown sugar

finely grated rind and juice of 2 large lemons

3 eggs, separated

250 g (9 oz) self-raising flour

10 ml (2 tsp) caraway seeds

175 g (6 oz) icing sugar, plus a little extra to decorate

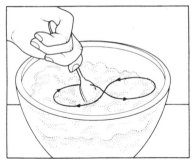

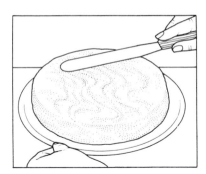

1 Grease and base-line an 18-cm (7-inch) round cake tin. In a bowl, cream together 175 g (6 oz) butter, the brown sugar and the rind from one lemon, until fluffy.

2 Beat in the egg yolks, then stir in flour, caraway seeds and 45 ml (3 tbsp) lemon juice.

3 Fold in the stiffly whisked egg whites; turn into tin. Bake in the oven at 180°C (350°F) mark 4 for 1 hour. Turn out onto a wire rack and leave to cool for 1 hour.

4 To make the butter icing, cream remaining butter until fluffy. Gradually sift in icing sugar until smooth. Beat in 15 ml (1 tbsp) lemon juice and the remaining grated lemon rind.

5 Use the lemon butter icing to completely coat the cake and then swirl using a small palette knife. Dust lightly with sifted icing sugar. Best eaten the next day.

CINNAMON CHOCOLATE TORTE

| 1.15* | £ £ | ✳* | 713–950 cals |

* plus 2 hours cooling; freeze after stage 4

Serves 6–8

| 175 g (6 oz) plain chocolate |
| 45 ml (3 tbsp) water |
| 175 g (6 oz) butter |
| 200 g (7 oz) caster sugar |
| 5 eggs, separated |
| 150 g (5 oz) flour |
| 15 ml (3 tsp) ground cinnamon |
| 75 g (3 oz) ground almonds |
| 90 ml (6 tbsp) apricot jam |
| 30 ml (2 tbsp) lemon juice |
| 300 ml (10 fl oz) whipping cream |
| icing sugar |

1 Grease and base-line two 19-cm (7½-inch) straight-sided sandwich tins. Put the chocolate and water in a small basin standing over a pan of hot water. Melt gently, then leave to cool.

2 Cream butter and sugar until light, beat in egg yolks. Add cooled chocolate, mix well.

3 Sift the flour with 10 ml (2 tsp) cinnamon and fold into the creamed mixture with ground almonds and whisked egg whites.

4 Spoon into the prepared tins and bake in the oven at 190°C (375°F) mark 5 for 35–40 minutes or until a skewer emerges clean and dry. Turn out and cool on a rack for about 2 hours.

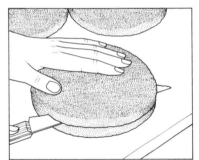

5 Split each cake in half. Put apricot jam in a small pan with lemon juice and remaining cinnamon and heat gently. Cool and spread on cakes. Layer up with cream and decorate top with sifted icing sugar just before serving.

CHOCOLATE

This is an adaptation of a German recipe—the word *torte* meaning cake—and the type of plain chocolate to use is the dark and rich continental variety. Most supermarkets and delicatessens sell French, Swiss or Belgian chocolate that is suitable for baking—they are not over-sweet and have excellent melting properties. For this cake, do not use the block or chips labelled 'cooking chocolate'—their flavour could ruin the finished cake.

POPPY SEED GRANARY ROUND

| 1.15* | ▯ | £ | ✳ | 280 cals |

* plus 1½ hours rising and proving

Makes 8 rolls

15 g (½ oz) fresh yeast or 7.5 g (¼ oz)
    dried yeast and 2.5 ml (½ tsp)
    sugar

300 ml (½ pint) warm water

450 g (1 lb) granary bread flour

5 ml (1 tsp) salt

50 g (2 oz) butter

50 g (2 oz) Cheddar cheese, grated

25 g (1 oz) poppy seeds

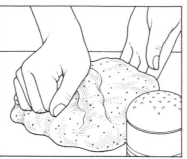

1 Grease a 20.5-cm (8-inch)
  sandwich tin. In a bowl,
crumble the fresh yeast into the
water and stir until dissolved. (If
using dried yeast, sprinkle it into
water mixed with the sugar. Leave
in a warm place for 15 minutes
until frothy.)

2 Make the dough. Place the
  flour and salt in a large bowl
and rub in the butter. Add the
cheese and the poppy seeds, reserving 5 ml (1 tsp) to garnish. Stir
in the yeast liquid and mix to a
stiff dough.

3 Turn on to a lightly floured
  surface and knead for 10 minutes until smooth. Place in a bowl,
cover with a cloth and leave to rise
in a warm place for about 1 hour
until doubled in size.

4 Turn on to a lightly floured
  surface and knead for 2–3
minutes until smooth.

5 Using a sharp knife, divide the
  dough into eight equal pieces
and shape into neat, even-sized
rolls with your hands.

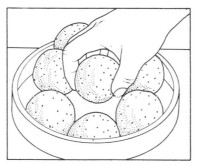

6 Arrange in the tin, cover with
  a clean cloth and leave to prove
in a warm place for about 30
minutes until doubled in size.

7 Sprinkle with the reserved
  poppy seeds. Bake in the oven
at 200°C (400°F) mark 6 for about
25 minutes until golden brown and
sounds hollow when the bottom of
the bread is tapped.

HERBY CHEESE LOAF

1.00*	£	1458 cals

* plus 1 hour cooling

Makes one 450-g (1-lb loaf)

225 g (8 oz) self-raising flour

7.5 ml (1½ tsp) salt

5 ml (1 tsp) mustard powder

5 ml (1 tsp) snipped fresh chives

15 ml (1 tbsp) chopped fresh parsley

75 g (3 oz) mature Cheddar cheese, grated

1 egg, beaten

150 ml (¼ pint) water

25 g (1 oz) butter or block margarine, melted

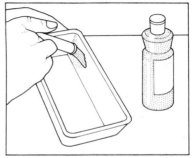

1 Grease a 450-g (1-lb) loaf tin. Sift the flour, salt and mustard into a bowl and stir in the herbs and cheese. Add the egg, water and melted fat and stir until well blended with a wooden spoon.

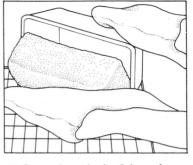

2 Spoon into the loaf tin and bake in the oven at 190°C (375°F) mark 5 for about 45 minutes. Turn out and cool on a wire rack for about 1 hour. Serve sliced and buttered while warm.

LEBKUCHEN

1.30* £ 92 cals*

* plus about 30 minutes cooling; calories are per biscuit

Makes about 40

175 g (6 oz) clear honey

50 g (2 oz) sugar

30 ml (2 tbsp) vegetable oil

30 ml (2 tbsp) water

1 egg yolk

5 ml (1 tsp) cocoa powder

6 drops of lemon oil

2.5 ml (½ tsp) ground cardamom

2.5 ml (½ tsp) ground cinnamon

1.25 ml (¼ tsp) ground cloves

good pinch of cayenne pepper

250 g (8 oz) flour

15 ml (3 tsp) baking powder

75 g (3 oz) ground almonds

75 g (3 oz) ground hazelnuts

75 g (3 oz) dried apricots, finely chopped

50 g (2 oz) cut mixed peel

175 g (6 oz) icing sugar

1 egg white

1 Put the honey, sugar, vegetable oil and water in a heavy saucepan and heat gently until melted. Leave until cold, then stir in the egg yolk, cocoa powder, lemon oil and spices.

2 Sift the flour and baking powder together. Add two-thirds of the flour to the spice mixture and stir well to mix.

3 Mix the remaining flour with the nuts, apricots and peel. Add to the spice mixture and mix well until combined.

4 Turn the dough out onto a floured surface and knead lightly until it comes together. Roll out until very thin (about 5 mm [¼ inch]) thick.

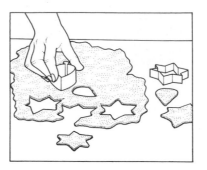

5 Stamp into about 40 shapes using fancy biscuit cutters. Re-roll any odd bits of pastry, if necessary.

6 Stamp out a small hole in some of the biscuits with an apple corer, drinking straw or skewer. Leave rest of biscuits plain.

7 Place the biscuit shapes on greased baking sheets and bake in batches in the oven at 170°C (325°F) mark 3 for 12–15 minutes until just beginning to colour. Transfer to a wire rack until cold and crisp.

8 Make the icing. Sift the icing sugar into a bowl, then beat in the egg white and 1–2 drops of warm water to make a thick spreading consistency.

9 Spread or pipe the icing immediately over the biscuits and leave on the wire rack to set for 2–3 hours.

10 Thread coloured ribbon through the holes in the biscuits and tie to secure.

LEBKUCHEN

These German biscuits are spicy and crisp—they are part of *Weinachtsbäckerei*, the famous collection of biscuits and small cakes that are traditional around Christmastime. They were originally baked in monasteries 700 years ago, when honey was used, because sugar was unknown in Europe at the time. The bakers who made these biscuits in 17th century Germany took their profession so seriously that they even formed a guild, calling themselves *Lebküchner*. There are many different kinds of lebkuchen, depending on the town or region where they are made, but the original recipe came from Nürnberg in Bavaria.

Commercially made lebkuchen are baked in special decorative moulds—the ones from Nürnberg have views of the town on them—and they are often iced with intricate patterns. When making lebkuchen at home, use as many different shapes of biscuit cutter that you can to add interest, and pipe glacé icing on them if you wish. In Germany they are also sometimes sprinkled with coloured sugar crystals or hundreds and thousands. When threaded with coloured ribbon or string, lebkuchen look pretty hanging on the Christmas tree.

MARMALADE SPICE CAKE

1.20* £ ✳	380–475 cals

* plus 1–2 hours cooling

Serves 8–10

175 g (6 oz) butter or block margarine, at room temperature
120 ml (8 tbsp) golden syrup
2 eggs, size 2, beaten
150 ml (10 tbsp) medium cut orange marmalade
350 g (12 oz) self-raising flour
5 ml (1 tsp) baking powder
5 ml (1 tsp) ground nutmeg
5 ml (1 tsp) ground cinnamon
1.25 ml ($\frac{1}{4}$ tsp) ground cloves
about 150 ml ($\frac{1}{4}$ pint) milk
50 g (2 oz) cornflakes

1 Grease and base-line a 20.5-cm (8-inch) square or 23-cm (9-inch) round cake tin.

2 In a bowl, beat the butter with 90 ml (6 tbsp) of the golden syrup until well mixed. Gradually beat in the eggs, keeping the mixture stiff.

3 Chop the marmalade and stir half into the cake mixture. Mix in the flour sifted with the baking powder and spices, adding sufficient milk to give a fairly stiff consistency. Turn into prepared cake tin, level the surface.

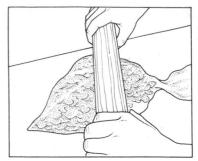

4 Crush the cornflakes and mix with the remaining syrup and marmalade. Carefully spread over the cake mixture.

5 Bake in the oven at 180°C (350°F) mark 4 for about 1 hour until well risen and firm. Turn out and cool on a wire rack for 1–2 hours before serving.

USEFUL INFORMATION
AND
BASIC RECIPES

Herbs, Spices and Other Flavourings

The term herb applies when leaves, flowers and sometimes the stem of a non-woody plant are used, either fresh or dried. A spice, on the other hand, refers to parts of an aromatic, often woody plant and may include the seeds, bark or roots. It is usually dried and then used either whole or ground. Herbs and spices can be used either individually or in combinations. See page 4 for information about stockists.

A–Z OF HERBS

ANGELICA
A tall plant that can be grown as a perennial or biennial. The bright green leaves are divided into large leaflets and the small yellow flowers grow in a ball-like cluster. The thick, hollow stems of angelica are candied and used to decorate desserts. The leaves can be used fresh in savoury dishes and both stems and leaves are used for herb teas.

BASIL
Basil is a delicate annual plant that survives only during the summer months. It has small, soft, oval leaves and tiny white flowers. It can be used fresh or dried, in most savoury dishes and is particularly good in those that contain tomatoes. It is also an essential ingredient in the famous Italian pesto sauce. Try it in soups, sauces and dressings, stuffings and casseroles.

BAY
Bay leaves come from an evergreen tree that can be kept small in pots or allowed to grow to full height in the open. The leaves are large, flat, oval and glossy. Used fresh but most often dried (the fresh leaves can sometimes taste rather bitter), bay leaves are tied into bouquets garnis, they can also be used alone (both whole and crumbled) to flavour sauces, soups and casserole dishes, as well as milk puddings, creams and custards. Always discard the whole bay leaves before serving.

BERGAMOT

Bergamot is a perennial plant, bushy and about 30 cm (12 inches) high. The leaves are broad and oval and the flowers large, red and shaggy. Bergamot is mostly used to make a herbal tea known as oswego tea, but it can also add a fresh flavour to summer drinks. Use sparingly in salads.

BORAGE

Borage is an annual plant with large, fleshy, hairy leaves and small blue flowers. The leaves have a delicate, cucumber like flavour and, when young, can be added to summer salads. They can also be candied. Both flowers and leaves can be added to summer drinks such as Pimm's, and the flowers are used to decorate fruit salads.

CHAMOMILE

Chamomile is an annual plant with feathery leaves and white, daisy-like flowers. It should not be confused with the low-growing lawn chamomile. Rarely used in cooking, chamomile's chief use is in making a delicate-flavoured, soothing tea (for which the dried flower-heads are used).

CHERVIL

Chervil is an annual plant, closely related to parsley. It has very delicate, lacy leaves with a hint of liquorice about their flavour. Because they are so delicate, large amounts of the fresh herb must be

used. Chervil can be used in fish dishes and herb butters, and is particularly good with eggs and with vegetables such as carrots. It also brings out the flavour of other herbs, and is used in *fines herbes* mixtures (see page 156).

CHIVES

Chives are a perennial member of the onion family. The thin, almost grass-like leaves grow in clumps and have a delicate, onion flavour. Snip them away with scissors and more will grow. Chives are often added to egg salads and omelettes and they are good with oily fish, in green summer salads and in herb butters. The tufted purple flowers are edible and make a pretty garnish.

COMFREY

Comfrey is a tall, perennial plant with clusters of purple, bell-like flowers and large, fleshy, hairy leaves. It is often used medicinally, but the fresh leaves can be cooked in butter or deep-fried and eaten as a vegetable. They can also be used (dried and powdered) in herbal teas and, when young, can be added to salads. In addition, the dried root is sometimes used to flavour country wines.

CORIANDER

Coriander is a highly aromatic annual plant, related to parsley. The fresh leaves are often used, scattered over Middle Eastern dishes and curries. They can also be used sparingly in salads and stuffings, and look good sprinkled over summer soups.

CURRY PLANT

The curry plant is a shrubby perennial plant that grows into a low spreading bush with green, spiky leaves. Although it is not used in authentic Indian curries, the leaves do have a strong curry-like flavour. Add them sparingly to winter soups and stews, to stuffings for game and to veal dishes. They can be used fresh or dried.

DILL WEED

Dill is an annual plant, related to parsley and growing quite tall with feathery leaves. These are referred to as dill weed so as to distinguish them from the seed (see spices). Dill is often used in cucumber salads and pickles. It is good with fish and summer vegetables, and in Scandinavia is an essential ingredient in the dish of salted raw salmon known as Gravlax. It is also macerated in wine vinegar to make dill vinegar.

FENNEL

Not to be confused with the bulbous stem vegetable, Florence fennel, the herb fennel is a very tall, perennial plant with large, feathery leaves and clusters of tiny yellow flowers. It has a fresh flavour reminiscent of liquorice and is most often used with fish. It is also very good in green and potato salads, and goes well with pork. The stems may be dried, broken into short lengths and placed under meat which is to be barbecued.

LAVENDER

Lavender is a well-loved, sweetly scented perennial plant with long, spear-like, grey-green leaves and spikes of purple flowers. Lavender is usually grown for its aromatic properties, but it can be added to mixtures of herbs for stews, casseroles and marinades for game. The flowers can be crystallised, used to make conserves or made into jelly.

LEMON BALM

This perennial plant is also known as balm or bee-balm. It has pale green, heart-shaped leaves which have a distinct lemony flavour. Use them in fish and poultry dishes, in sauces, marinades and stuffings. They can be added to salads, cream cheese, fruit salads and milk puddings, and will make a refreshing addition to summer fruit cups as well as a soothing tea.

LEMON VERBENA

Lemon verbena is a perennial plant that likes a warm, sunny situation. It is a tall shrub with long, pale green, pointed, lemon-scented leaves, which can be used in stuffings (sparingly) and to flavour fish and poultry. Add them to fruit salads and sweet puddings, or use them to flavour wine cups and to make a refreshing tea.

LOVAGE

A medicinal as well as a culinary herb, lovage grows very tall, with dark, shiny leaves and clusters of yellow flowers. It has a  celery-like flavour, which adds a sharp spiciness to casseroles and soups, as well as green salads and omelettes.

MARJORAM

Although there are two varieties of marjoram (sweet and wild), the name marjoram is usually applied to the sweet—the  wild being more commonly referred to as oregano (see right). Sweet marjoram is a low-growing perennial plant with small, oval leaves. It has a spicy, slightly sweet flavour that will enhance rather than mask delicate flavours. Marjoram is often tied into bouquets garnis, and is used to flavour soups and stews. It is good with pork, veal and poultry, eggs and vegetables; and also in milk drinks and puddings.

MINT

There are many different varieties of this perennial, oval-leaved plant. The one most used is *spearmint*. It is a favourite accompaniment  to lamb, and is made into mint jelly and a mint sauce with vinegar. Add a sprig to new potatoes and green peas as they cook and scatter chopped fresh mint over them for serving. Add chopped mint to salads (both sweet and savoury) and to Middle Eastern tabbouleh. *Applemint* has rounded slightly furry leaves. As its name implies, it has a slight

apple flavour. It makes delicious mint sauce and jelly and a sprig added to apple jelly as it cooks will improve the flavour. Chopped applemint leaves can be added to fresh fruit salads or sprinkled over cut grapefruit. *Peppermint* has dark green, shiny leaves with a hint of purple. Oil distilled from them contains menthol and is used to flavour confectionery, liqueurs and toothpaste. The chopped leaves can be added to fruit salads and made jellies, sauces and peppermint tea.

OREGANO

Also known as wild marjoram, oregano is a perennial plant. It has a more pungent, spicy flavour than sweet marjoram (see left) and it is much used in Italian cooking, adding interest to pasta dishes and pizzas. It also makes a good addition to vegetable dishes, particularly those containing tomatoes, aubergines, courgettes and sweet peppers. It is nearly always used dried.

PARSLEY

Parsley is probably the most used of all herbs. It is a biennial plant with bright green leaves which can either be curled (English parsley) or flat (Continental parsley). It is always included in bouquets garnis and *fines herbes*. It can be used too as a garnish for all savoury dishes and can be chopped into salads and herb butters. It can also be used to make parsley sauce, and tartare and Ravigote sauce and is excellent with fish and seafood, with veal, poultry, eggs and vegetables.

ROSEMARY

Rosemary is a perennial, shrubby bush, the leaves of which can be picked all through the year. They are small  and spiked, dark green on one side and grey-green on the other. Rosemary has a strong, pungent flavour. It may overpower other herbs, so is best used on its own to flavour lamb, pork and poultry, root vegetables and fish. In small quantities it can also be used to flavour bread rolls and scones. It is available fresh, as dried leaves or in powder form.

RUE

Rue is a perennial herb with a woody stem and small, blue-green, irregularly cut leaves. It has a slightly bitter flavour so should  be used sparingly. Add tiny amounts of the chopped leaves to salads and a small pinch to cream or cottage cheese or egg for sandwiches. It is dangerous to use rue in large quantities as some people are allergic to it.

SAGE

Sage is a perennial herb with grey-green, oval leaves. It has been used for centuries to flavour and counteract the  richness of fatty meats such as pork, goose and duck. It has also been used to flavour cheese and can be put into cheese dishes. It is often included in a bouquet garni and can be added to casseroles, stews, stuffings and sausages.

SALAD BURNET

Salad burnet is a perennial herb, its leaves grow in a fountain-shaped clump. Each has a red stem with six or more pairs of round leaflets on either side. Salad burnet has a slightly bitter, cucumber-like flavour and the young leaves can be added to salads and used to flavour vinegar. It can also be added to vegetable dishes and soups and stuffings.

SAVORY

There are two types of savory, the perennial winter and the annual summer savory. They look similar with small, spiky dull-green leaves. Both have a peppery flavour, but that of summer savory is fresher. Both types are good with pork and can be added to beef casseroles, egg dishes, tomato-flavoured sauces and veal pies. Summer savory is known as 'the bean herb'. Add it to both broad and runner beans.

SORREL

For flavour and delicacy of texture, choose French sorrel with its shiny, large, spear-shaped leaves. It is a perennial plant and can be picked for most of the year. It can be used to make the delicately-flavoured sorrel soup and also in omelettes, sauces and stuffings (particularly with fish). The raw leaves can be chopped and added to salads and can also be cooked alone as a vegetable.

SWEET CICELY

Sweet cicely is a tall, attractive perennial plant with ferny leaves and clusters of tiny white flowers. The leaves have a sweet, aniseed-like flavour. Add them to green salads and salad dressings, omelettes and pancakes. They are also delicious sprinkled into fruit salads, and act as both sweetener and flavouring when cooked with tart fruits. Sweet cicely is often used as a flavouring for liqueurs.

TANSY

A tall perennial plant with ferny, dark-green leaves and button-like yellow flowers. Use the youngest leaves as they are the most tender. Traditionally, chopped tansy has been added to omelettes, but it can also be put into stuffings, casseroles and sausages. With the chopped leaves of sage and mint, it makes a delicious herb butter.

TARRAGON

The best culinary variety is French tarragon. It is a perennial which dies down in autumn and has narrow, green shiny leaves and a spicy flavour. Russian tarragon is less spicy. Tarragon is often used in chicken dishes and is an essential ingredient in Béarnaise, Tartare and Hollandaise sauces and in *fines herbes*. It can also be used to make herb butter and added to salads.

THYME

The low-growing, perennial thyme with its tiny, dull green leaves is a favourite in most herb gardens. Tie it into bouquets garnis and use it in soups, stuffings, casseroles and sauces. It goes well with all meats and can be added to a court bouillon for poaching fish. Use the chopped leaves to make herb butter, add them to bread and scone doughs and use them to make a jelly to serve with roast meats.

Lemon thyme is a variety of thyme. A low-growing perennial with tiny, shiny leaves on woody stems, its flavour is that of lemon with strong undertones of thyme. Use it with fish dishes, and also with lamb and veal. Add the leaves to fruit salads and put a sprig into the pan when scalding milk or cream for sweet dishes.

WOODRUFF

Woodruff is a delicate, perennial plant with small, spiked leaves growing in whirls around the delicate stems. The white star-like flowers grow on the top ruff of leaves. Woodruff has a vanilla-like scent and can be used like a vanilla pod. Steep the leaves in milk before making custard or pastry cream, or add it to the saucepan while you are scalding cream to make ice-cream.

A–Z OF SPICES

AJOWAN

Small, light brown, slightly elongated seeds which have a rather coarse flavour of thyme, ajowan is a spice related to caraway and cumin. It is used most often in Indian cookery, both to flavour food and to counteract the effect of ingredients such as pulses which can cause flatulence. It is also used medicinally to relieve stomach upsets.

ALLSPICE

Also known as Jamaica pepper, the seeds of all-spice are just slightly larger than peppercorns and dark brown in colour. Despite its alternative name it is not peppery in flavour, but delicately spicy with a tinge of cloves, cinnamon and nutmeg. Allspice can be bought whole or ground and it can be added to both sweet and savoury dishes. Add ground all-spice to ginger cakes and scald whole seeds in milk for making puddings and custards. It is also an ingredient in pickling spice and is used in salting meats.

ANISEED

The tiny, purse-shaped seeds of anise have a warm, sweet, pungent flavour and can be used in sweet and savoury dishes. Add them to cakes, biscuits and confectionery, to the syrups of fruit salads and to syllabubs and custards. Their flavour also goes well with fish and pork, vegetables and cream cheese.

ANISE PEPPER

Used mainly in Chinese cookery, anise pepper is also known as Chinese pepper and Szechuan pepper. It consists of small, round red-brown, rough-coated berries which have a hot, spicy flavour. It is used in the warming dishes of northern China and goes with fish, chicken and lamb. When ground and dry-fried with salt it is used as a condiment for seafood. Anise pepper is one of the ingredients of five-spice powder (see page 139).

CARAWAY

The small, elongated, dark brown seeds of caraway have a warming but slightly sharp flavour. Their valuable digestive properties make them particularly suitable for eating with rich, fatty foods such as pork, but they are also excellent added to cabbage dishes and sauerkraut. Most often, however, they are added to cakes and pastries and baked apples. In Germany they are used to flavour cheese and are an ingredient in some liqueurs.

CARDAMOM

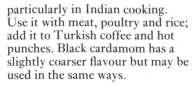

Available as pods and seeds, carda-mom comes from a perennial plant related to ginger. The pods (which contain the seeds) can be either green or black. Cardamom seeds should always be bought inside their pods, removed by crushing and discarding the pods, and ground at home as, once ground, their light, sweet, sherbety flavour is quickly lost. Green cardamom has the finer flavour and is added to both sweet and savoury dishes, particularly in Indian cooking. Use it with meat, poultry and rice; add it to Turkish coffee and hot punches. Black cardamom has a slightly coarser flavour but may be used in the same ways.

CASSIA

Related to cinnamon. The dried bark, the dried unripe seeds and the dried leaves are all used in cookery. The bark has a similar flavour to cinnamon but is not as strong; it may be used in the same way as cinnamon sticks. The seeds, sometimes known as Chinese cassia buds, are used in drinks and confectionery and are added to pots pourris.

CAYENNE PEPPER

Derived from a hot, red variety of the capsicum family. The pods are small, long and narrow and, when picked and dried, both pods and seeds are ground together. Cayenne pepper has a clean, sharp flavour and is used for flavouring seafood in many parts of the world. It is also added to Indian curries and the spiced stews of the Middle East, as well as the classic brown and Hollandaise sauces in Western cooking.

CELERY SEEDS

The tiny, light brown, slightly elongated seeds of celery have a bitter, celery flavour and therefore should be used sparingly in soups and casseroles. Add them to a court bouillon for poaching fish and to pickle mixtures for vegetables and seafood. A small pinch will enliven a salad dressing; they can also be added to bread rolls.

CHILLIES

Small varieties of capsicum with a specially hot flavour. *Whole dried chillies* are added to pickling spice and are used for flavouring spiced vinegars. They can be finely chopped and added to hot spiced dishes when fresh chillies are not available. The seeds are the hottest part, so if you want a less fiery flavouring, omit these. Always wash your hands thoroughly after handling chillies. *Chilli powder* is made by grinding dried red chillies and has a clean, fresh, hot taste. It is added to Indian curries, spiced Middle Eastern dishes and used in Caribbean and Creole cookery. It is good with seafood and in sauces. *Chili Seasoning* consists of chilli powder that has been mixed with oregano, chocolate, cumin and other flavourings. It is often used in Mexican dishes and is popular in the United States. *Fresh chillies* are small and tapering and should look smooth and shiny. They are sold either unripe (green) or ripe (red). They have a hot flavour and are used in curries and other hot dishes; they can also be added very sparingly to salads made from dried pulses. Core and seed them before use, although a few seeds can be left in if a very hot, pungent effect is needed for a particular recipe.

CINNAMON

Native to Ceylon, cinnamon is the bark of a tree which is a member of the laurel family. The bark is peeled from the young shoots of the tree, then left to dry in the sun so that it curls into quills, known as cinnamon sticks. The bark of the cassia tree is often sold as cinnamon, which it resembles closely, both in flavour and appearance. Known for centuries for its fragrant and therapeutic qualities, cinnamon has many uses in cooking. Use the sticks to infuse flavour into drinks, pickles, fruit compotes, milk puddings and casseroles. Ground cinnamon is best for cakes and puddings—it has a special affinity with chocolate.

CLOVES

The name clove comes from the Latin word for nail, *clavus*, which the spice resembles in appearance. Cloves are in fact the flower buds of an evergreen shrub native to the Moluccas or Spice Islands, but nowadays the majority are imported from Zanzibar and Madagascar. The volatile oil of cloves is a powerful antiseptic (it is a standard remedy for toothache) and cloves are also used in the making of pomanders. In cooking, cloves are used both in their whole and ground form. Whole cloves are most often used in marinades for meat and fish, and for infusing pickles and hot drinks; they are also used for studding whole onions and hams. Use ground cloves in baking and puddings, particularly with apples.

CORIANDER

Round, light brown seeds with a fresh, spicy flavour. They can be bought whole or ground and are used in many Indian and Pakistani dishes. Their flavour is improved if they are gently dry-roasted before grinding. Use coriander in curries and put the whole seeds into vegetables à la grecque. Ground coriander can be added to bread and cakes. The spice is an ingredient in liqueurs and vermouths.

CUMIN

Small, dark brown, elongated seeds with a rich, dry flavour.  Cumin is frequently used in Indian and Middle Eastern dishes. In European cooking the whole seeds are sometimes used in pickling. A sweet, spicy drink is made with cumin, ginger and tamarind, but apart from this cumin is not used in sweet dishes.

DILL

The oval, flattened seeds of the dill plant are dried and used whole as a spice. Use them in pickles and sprinkle them sparingly into salads. They can be added to cabbage and to dishes of braised root vegetables. Like caraway seeds, they can be added to cake mixtures, buns and confectionery.

FENNEL SEEDS

The tiny, purselike seeds of fennel have a warm, slightly bitter, aniseed flavour. They have strong digestive qualities 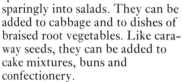 and so are often used with rich meats and oily fish. Sprinkle them over mackerel or herrings before grilling. Add them to pork and creamy sauces. They can also be used to flavour pickles and added to bread and cakes. Fennel is also used occasionally to flavour curries.

FENUGREEK

Small, hard, yellow-brown seeds. To remove their slightly bitter taste, fry them in hot oil before using until they brown.  Whole or ground fenugreek is used in the cooking of Mediterranean countries, but is most often used in Indian curries. The whole, untreated seeds can be used to flavour pickles; they can also be sprouted and used in salads, providing an excellent source of vitamin E.

GINGER

Dried ginger root can be bought whole, taking the form of small, fibrous, light-coloured pieces about 2.5–5 cm (1–2 inches) long;  or ground in the form of a light, beige-coloured powder. The whole pieces should be bruised before being used in pickling. *Ground ginger* is often used to flavour cakes, biscuits, puddings, wines and cordials. *Fresh ginger root* has a warm, citrus-like flavour. It is usually peeled and grated or finely chopped and used to flavour fish, poultry, soups and casseroles. It is also added to curries and other oriental and South-east Asian dishes. Try it in marinades for chicken and fish.

JUNIPER

Round, purple-brown berries, about twice the size of peppercorns with smooth skins.  They are always bought whole and are easy to grind as they are soft. Juniper berries are often included in spice mixtures for meat and are excellent with pork and game. They can be added to casseroles and pâtés, and are also good with cabbage. Juniper berries are an important flavouring ingredient in gin.

LAOS POWDER

Closely related to ginger and is similar in that the root is the part used. It has a peppery ginger taste and is used in the hot dishes of Southeast Asia. In Europe it is used to flavour liqueurs and bitters. It is also known as galangal or galingale.

MACE

Mace blades form the outer casing of the nutmeg (see right). They are bright red when harvested and dry to a deep orange. Mace can be bought whole in the form of small lacy orange pieces or blades, or ground to an orange powder. The flavour is similar to nutmeg, but more delicate. Blades of mace are often used to flavour sauces. Ground mace is added to stuffings, pâtés, soups, stews, cheese sauces and cakes.

MUSTARD SEED

There are three types of mustard seed, black, brown and white. *Black mustard* is grown in only a few areas in Europe. *Brown mustard* has a similar flavour and is used in most English mustard mixes. *White mustard* is used mostly in American mixed mustards. Whole mustard seeds are used in pickling and can also be used in stuffings, sausages and certain curried dishes—particularly those containing spinach. They are increasingly being used in spiced grainy mustards.

English Mustard Powder was once made from ground black mustard seeds, but since these have become more scarce it is made from brown mustard with a little white mustard added. Also added are ground turmeric and wheat flour. To mix, add warm water to make a fine paste and leave for 10 minutes. Mustard powder has numerous uses in cooking, wherever a hot flavour is called for.

NUTMEG

Bought whole, as a small, oval, shiny nut, or ground. If bought whole, grate it only as you need it using a special nutmeg grater or other fine grater.

Nutmeg can be used in sweet and savoury dishes. Add it to puddings, cakes and biscuits and grate it over milk puddings. Use it with vegetables (particularly spinach); in sausages and stuffings and Middle Eastern spiced dishes; and in punches and night-time drinks.

PEPPER

Available whole or ground. Black and white peppercorns come from a tropical vine. To produce *black pepper* the berries are picked when green and dried whole. For *white pepper*, they are allowed to ripen and turn red and the skin is removed before drying. White pepper has a milder flavour than black. It is used in delicately flavoured dishes and light-coloured sauces and mayonnaise. Black pepper is used in most savoury dishes and can also be used in desserts. *Green peppercorns*: Some peppercorns are picked when still green and pickled in brine or vinegar or in their own juices.

These can be used whole or

coarsely crushed, and give a hot 'pickle' taste to recipes. They are used to flavour most meats and game (but particularly steak and duck) pâtés and sausages and savoury butters. Green peppercorns also go well with fresh strawberries.

Pink peppercorns are totally unrelated to the black peppercorn family, but come from a completely different plant, sometimes known as Brazilian pepper. Although they enjoyed some popularity a few years ago, this was short-lived as it was discovered that they can cause an allergic reaction.

POPPY SEED

Sometimes called maw seeds, these are derived from the opium poppy. The most common type in Europe is called black poppy seed, although in colour the tiny round seeds are blue-grey. The type used in India has a smaller, creamy-yellow seed. Both have a distinct nutty flavour.

Poppy seed is used in curries, but most often is sprinkled over breads and used as a filling in cakes and pastries.

SAFFRON

The tiny dried stigmas of the saffron crocus, this is the most expensive spice in the world. The stigmas or strands of saffron should be a brilliant orange colour and have a pungent, bitter taste.

Ground saffron is usually cheaper, but does not have such a good flavour and varies enormously in quality.

Saffron is used extensively in Indian and Mediterranean cooking and to flavour many rice dishes such as pilafs and paella, soups and fish dishes.

SESAME

Tiny, flat, oval seeds which may be red, light brown or black. They have a rich, nutty flavour and are often sprinkled over breads. They can also be toasted and used in salads and sprinkled over hot spiced dishes. A nutty flavoured edible oil is derived from sesame seeds. They are also ground to produce a rich grey paste known as tahini, which is used for dips, a dip of chick peas called hummus.

STAR ANISE

The star-shaped fruit of an evergreen tree native to southwest China. When dried it is a red-brown colour and the flavour is one of pungent aniseed.

In China, star anise is used to flavour stewed and simmered dishes, particularly those of duck, beef, chicken and lamb. It is also placed under whole fish for steaming. It is used whole and one star is quite sufficient to flavour a large dish. Star anise is one of the ingredients of five-spice powder (see page 139).

TURMERIC

Related to ginger and the part used is the knobbly rhizome, which is bright orange inside the peel. Whole pieces of turmeric can be bought, but this is one spice that is most frequently bought ground.

Use it quickly as its flavour deteriorates on keeping. Turmeric is used in curries and curry powder and is added to mustards and pickles. Its bright colour makes it useful for colouring rice and sweet Indian dishes.

VANILLA

The pod of a type of orchid, yellow-green when picked and dark brown after curing and drying. The pod can  be re-used several times provided it is dried well and stored in a polythene bag.

Vanilla is essentially a flavouring for sweet dishes particularly ice creams, custards and pastry cream. Use it to flavour hot chocolate or coffee drinks and infuse it in wine cups. Keep it permanently in a jar of caster sugar to make your own vanilla sugar.

GRINDING YOUR OWN SPICES

Spices taste better when freshly ground. Peppercorns and allspice berries can have their own peppermills. Small amounts of spice can be crushed with a pestle and mortar or with a rolling pin. Grind large amounts in an electric or hand grinder, remembering to wipe it out well each time with kitchen paper, so that no cross flavouring occurs. Most spices benefit from being gently dry-fried for a few minutes before being ground. This releases extra flavour, especially with spices such as cumin and coriander. To dry-fry spices, see page 139.

OTHER FLAVOURINGS

ASAFOETIDA

This is not a true spice but is derived from the resin of a plant native to Afghanistan and Iran. It can be bought in solid form but as it is very hard is best bought ground, in powder form. The flavour is pungent, a little like spicy garlic. Like ajowan, it is used to counteract flatulence. Asafoetida is used in very small quantities, mainly in Indian cooking for pickles, fish and vegetables. In India, it is often used as a substitute for salt.

CAPERS

The pickled buds of the caper bush that grows wild around the Mediterranean. Capers are dull green, pointed at one end and with a  pungent pickle flavour. They are used with fish and in sauces such as Tartare, Remoulade and Ravigote. They can also be used to flavour butter and as a garnish, sprinkled over salads and seafood.

COCONUT MILK

The coconut milk referred to in many recipes has nothing to do with the natural 'milk' or juice in the centre of the coconut, but is actually made using either fresh coconut or creamed coconut (sold in compressed block form in supermarkets and delicatessens). In Indian and Southeast Asian dishes, it gives a subtle, creamy flavour and takes the harsh 'edge' off hot, fiery spices. To make coconut milk, see recipe on page 157.

GARLIC

Garlic is a perennial plant that is more often grown as an annual. It is a member of the onion family and has small, white, oval-shaped bulbs or cloves held together in a cluster by a white outer skin. Garlic will enhance most savoury dishes: add it to salads, soups, casseroles, pâtés, sauté dishes and roasts.

Garlic is readily available dried and powdered, and is a convenient substitute for fresh garlic in soups and savoury dishes.

GERANIUM

The geraniums most used for culinary purposes are the rose-scented, mint-scented and lemon-scented varieties. Put leaves into the base of a cake tin when making a sponge cake and remove them when the cake is cooked. When making custard add them to the pan when scalding the milk. They can also be used to flavour milk puddings, sweet sauces, sorbets, jellies, jams and herb teas.

HORSERADISH

The grated root of the horseradish plant is available dried in jars. Use it as for fresh. Horseradish, related to mustard, is a perennial plant, of which the long tapering, creamy coloured root is used. Lift the roots in Autumn, scrub and grate them and preserve them in jars, covered with wine vinegar. Use horseradish to make a creamy sauce for roast beef. Add it to beetroot or cucumber salads and to vinaigrette dressings. Sprinkle it over mackerel fillets before grilling.

LEMON GRASS

Lemon grass is grown mostly in tropical and subtropical countries but is imported to the West, in fresh and dried forms and as a powder  (sereh powder: see page 4 for stockists). It has thick, grass-like leaves which smell and taste strongly of lemon. It is most often used in the cooking of Sri Lanka and Southeast Asia to flavour curry and meat dishes. It can also be used with fish and to flavour sweet puddings.

ROSE

Both the petals and hips of sweet scented roses can be used for culinary purposes. The petals can be crystallised and made into jam.  Rose vinegar (made from rose petals infused in wine vinegar) adds a delicate flavour to salads and you can make rose petal wine. Rose hips are an excellent source of vitamin C. Make them into syrup or rose hip jelly. Probably the most common use of roses in cooking, however, is in rosewater, used to flavour and perfume many Middle Eastern sweets and confections.

TAMARIND

Tamarind is the large pod that grows on the Indian tamarind tree. After picking, it is seeded, peeled and pressed into a dark-brown pulp.

It is used to add a sour flavour to chutneys, sauces and curries, to which it is added in the form of tamarind juice. To make tamarind juice, see recipe on page 157.

VIOLET

Sweet violets grow wild and can also be cultivated. The violet is a tiny perennial plant with heart-shaped leaves and sweet-scented mauve or white flowers. The petals can be crystallised and used to decorate confectionery. They can also be used to make an unusual vinegar to flavour all kinds of sauces and stews. The petals are placed in a glass bottle to about one-third full and then topped up with red or white wine vinegar. The bottle is sealed and left in a warm place for two to three weeks before straining for use. The petals are also steeped in white wine cups.

DRY-FRYING SPICES

Dry-frying will mellow the flavour of spices. They can be dried singly or in mixtures. If mixing the spices, put the hardest ones such as fenugreek into the pan first and add softer ones such as coriander and cumin after a few minutes.

Heat a heavy frying pan over moderate heat. Put in the spices and stir them constantly until they are an even brown (do not allow them to burn). Tip the spices out to cool and then grind them in an electric grinder.

In China, a mixture of anise pepper and salt is roasted in this way to be used as a condiment for seafood and poultry.

HERB AND SPICE MIXTURES

BOUQUET GARNI

This is a small bunch of herbs, tied together with string so it can be suspended in soups, casseroles and sauté dishes and removed before serving. The classic ingredients are bay, parsley and thyme, but other herbs can be added to suit a particular dish. When dried herbs are used for a bouquet garni they are tied in a small muslin bag. To make a bouquet garni, see page 156.

CURRY POWDER

The flavourings for authentic Indian curries are made up of different mixtures of ground spices which include cumin, coriander, chilli powder and other aromatics.

You can mix your own (see page 156), but for speed, bought curry powders are available. Besides using it in ethnic dishes, curry powder can add spice to many other types of dishes.

Add it to salad dressings, sprinkle it into sauces and casseroles, and rub it into chicken skin before poaching.

FINES HERBES

This is a mixture of the finely chopped or dried leaves of parsley, chervil, chives and tarragon. To make *fines herbes*, see recipe on page 156.

FIVE-SPICE POWDER

A ground mixture of star anise, anise pepper, fennel seed, cloves and cinnamon or cassia. Five-spice powder is used in authentic Chinese cookery. It is cocoa coloured and very pungent and should be used sparingly. Five-spice powder is used to season Chinese red-cooked meats (meats simmered in soy sauce) and roast meats and poultry. It can also be added to marinades and sprinkled over whole steamed fish and vegetable dishes. To make five-spice powder, see recipe on page 156.

GARAM MASALA

A mixture of spices used in Indian cookery. It most frequently contains black pepper, cumin, cinnamon, black or green cardamoms, cloves and bay leaves. To make garam masala, see recipe on page 156.

HARISSA

Harissa is a hot mixture of chilli and other spices that is used in Middle Eastern cooking. It can be bought in powder and paste form and may contain up to twenty spices. It is often served with couscous and other North African dishes: it is put into a separate bowl, stock from the main dish is poured in to dilute it and it is spooned back over the dish to taste. To make harissa, see recipe on page 154.

MIXED SPICE

This is a mixture of sweet-flavoured ground spices. The main ingredient is nutmeg and included in smaller amounts are cinnamon, cloves, ginger, cardamom, vanilla, allspice and sometimes fennel seed.

Mixed spice is most often used in sweet dishes, cakes, biscuits and confectionery, but it can be added sparingly to curries and spiced Middle Eastern dishes. To make mixed spice, see recipe on page 156.

PICKLING SPICE

Pickling spice is a pungent mixture of varying spices, usually based on black peppercorns, red chillis and varying proportions of mustard seed, allspice, cloves, ginger, mace and coriander seed. To make pickling spice, see recipe on page 156.

NAME	STARTERS AND SOUPS	MAIN COURSES AND VEGETABLES	DESSERTS AND BAKING
AJOWAN	Curry-flavoured soups	Curries containing pulses, meat, vegetables	None
ALLSPICE	Beef and minestrone soups; pickles	Baked ham; beef stews; carrots; creamed potatoes; meat loaves; spiced meats	Apple pies and crumbles; cakes; fruit salads; milk puddings; stewed fruits
ANGELICA	Seafood salads	Baked or grilled fish; carrot, pea, and potato salads; use leaves as vegetables	Candied stems for decoration; cheesecake; cooked with sharp fruits; preserves
ANISEED	Cheese dips; cream soups; seafood	Carrots; courgettes; cucumber and green salads; fish; marrow; pork; poultry	Biscuits; cakes; confectionery; fresh fruit, especially figs; syrup for fruit salads
ANISE PEPPER	Fish and seafood	Steamed fish and chicken; Chinese dishes	None
ASAFOETIDA	Fish; pickles	Indian curries containing pulses	None
BASIL	Bouillabaisse and other fish soups; gazpacho; seafood; pesto sauce; tomato soup	Fish dishes; herb butter; meat casseroles; pasta; stuffings for poultry; tomato and green salads	Chop and add to flour for pastry for sweet pies
BAY	Aspics; soups; stocks	Meat, fish and vegetable dishes	Flavour milk for rice puddings
BERGAMOT	Flavour cream cheese; summer drinks	Salads; stuffings	Apple jelly; crystallise; herbal tea; sweet batters
BORAGE	Deep-fried in batter	Green salads	Herbal teas; summer drinks
BOUQUET GARNI	Aspics; meat and vegetable soups; stocks	Braised vegetables; casseroles; most meats, poultry and game; poached fish; sauces; stews	None
CARAWAY	Cream cheese; dips; seafood, pickles; vegetable soups	Beetroot; cabbage dishes; coleslaw and other salads; offal, pork; potatoes; tomatoes; veal	Biscuits; bread; cakes; pastries
CARDAMOM	Green pea soups; melon; pickling; spiced and curried soups	Curries and spiced dishes; rice	Bread; buns; custards; fruit salads; stewed and baked fruit; yeast cakes
CASSIA	Pickles; spiced drinks	Chinese dishes; curries; ground sprinkled over vegetables; rice	Poached fruits; stewed fruits
CAYENNE PEPPER	Fish soups and chowders; seafood salads; tomato soup	Curried vegetables; curries and other spiced meat dishes; egg dishes; fish dishes; salad dressings	None
CELERY SEED	Fish and meat soups; pickle mixtures; seafood	Casseroles; coleslaw; fish; salad dressings; sauces; stews	Bread; savoury biscuits
CHAMOMILE	Flavour sherry	None	Herbal tea
CHERVIL	Fish; fish soups; herb butters; seafood; vegetable soups	Chicken; cucumber; egg and cheese dishes; fish; meat sauces and casseroles; root vegetables; salads	Breads and savoury biscuits
CHILLI: fresh	Hot, spiced soups; seafood	Curries and hot, spiced dishes; egg dishes; pulses; salads	None
dried	Pickles	Curries and hot dishes; vinegar for salads	None
powder	Dips; fish soups and chowders; pickles; seafood	Barbecue sauce; curries and hot spiced dishes; eggs; fish; Creole dishes; poultry; salad dressings; veal	None
CHIVES	Chilled soups; dips	Egg, cheese and fish dishes; garnish for potato dishes; herb butters; salads; stuffings for poultry	None
COMFREY	Fritters	Cooked as vegetable; salads	Herbal tea
CORIANDER leaf	Dips; pickles; seafood; sprinkle over chilled soups	Salads; scattered over curries and Middle Eastern dishes; stuffings	None
seed	Seafood; spiced and chilled soups; yogurt dips	Curried vegetables; curries and mild spiced meat dishes; pulses; rubbed over pork or poultry before roasting; salad dressings; stuffings	Biscuits; cakes; fruit salads; stewed fruits
CUMIN SEED	Chutneys; pickles; spiced soup	Beef; cabbage; carrots; chicken; curries; kebabs; lamb; marinades; pulses; rice dishes	None
CURRY PLANT	Fish soups; seafood; spiced soups	Casseroles and stews; stuffings for veal and game	None
CURRY POWDER	Cream and cottage cheese; dips; seafood	Curried dishes; hot sauces; rice; salad dressings; sauces for eggs; white fish	Savoury bread and biscuits
DILL SEED	Light vegetable soups; pickles	Cabbage; carrots; casseroles of lamb and pork; cucumber; marrow; poached and baked fish; salad dressings; turnips	Biscuits; sprinkle over bread and buns
DILL WEED	Cheese dips; seafood; summer soups	Cauliflower; cucumber; kidneys; salads; salmon and other fish; sauces for fish; veal, pork	None
FENNEL leaf	Fish soups; seafood; summer soups	Chicken; eggs; fish; pork; salads and dressings; stuffings	None
seed	Pickles; seafood	Casseroles; chicken; herrings; mackerel; potatoes; salad dressings; sauces for fish	Biscuits; cakes; cooked apple dishes
FENUGREEK	Pickles	Indian and Middle Eastern dishes; sprouted in salads	None
FINES HERBES	All meat soups; dips	Butters; casseroles; egg dishes; stuffings	None
FIVE SPICE POWDER	Marinades; steamed fish	Chinese simmered meat dishes; Chinese stir-fried vegetables; roast meats and poultry	None
GARAM MASALA	Seafood	Indian dishes	None
GARLIC	Cream cheese dips; vegetable and meat soups	All meats and poultry; casseroles and stews; marinades; salad dressings; sautée dishes	None
GERANIUM, SCENTED	Cream cheese dips	Vinegars for salads	Cakes; jams; jellies; milk puddings; sauces; sugar; syrup for fruit salads; teas
GINGER, FRESH	Seafood	Chicken; curries; fish; marinades	None
GINGER, DRIED	Whole root in pickles	Baked ham; fish; pot roasts; pulses; rice	Cakes and biscuits; fruit pies; puddings; spiced drinks; stewed fruit
HORSERADISH	Sauce with smoked mackerel and trout	Salad dressings for potatoes and beetroot; sauce with beef; sauce with fish and hot beetroot	None
JUNIPER BERRIES	Pâtés; pickles; seafood	Baked ham; cabbage; casseroles; game; pork; pot roasts; poultry; salted meats	Spiced drinks containing gin; stewed apples

NAME	STARTERS AND SOUPS	MAIN COURSES AND VEGETABLES	DESSERTS AND BAKING
LAOS POWDER	Seafood	Southeast Asian dishes	None
LAVENDER	Game soup	Casseroles, particularly beef, game and poultry; marinades for game; stews	Conserves; crystallised flowers; jellies
LEMON BALM	Cream cheese dips; fish soups; seafood	Fish; green salads; marinades; poultry; sauces; stuffings; veal	Flavour sugar; fruit salads; herbal tea; milk puddings; summer drinks
LEMON GRASS	Seafood	Curried dishes; fish; salads	Milk puddings; sponge puddings; syrup for fruit salads
LEMON THYME	Cream cheese dips; seafood	Casseroles; chicken; fish; grills; herb butters; lamb; marinades; salads; sautée dishes; veal	Fruit salads; milk for custards and puddings
LEMON VERBENA	Seafood	Fish; green and rice salads; poultry; stuffings and sauces; veal	Flavour sugar; fruit salads; herbal tea; sweet puddings; wine cup
LOVAGE	Dips; pickles; seafood; vegetable and meat soups	Casseroles; green salads; poultry; stuffings	None
MACE	Pickles; seafood	Beef; chicken; meatballs; meat loaves; pâtés; pork; sauces; stuffings; veal	Biscuits; cakes; whipped cream
MARJORAM	Vegetable and meat soups	Casseroles; grilled meats; herb butters; sauces; stuffings; tomatoes	Flavour sugar; herbal teas
MINT (SPEARMINT)	Cream cheese dips; grapefruit; sprinkled over melon; summer soups; yogurt drinks	Lamb roasts and grills; mackerel; mint sauce; new carrots; peas; potatoes; salads; stuffings; trout	Blackcurrants; fruit salads; ice creams; summer drinks
MIXED SPICE	Melon	Curries and spiced dishes	Biscuits; cakes; drinks; fruit salads; stewed fruits
MUSTARD powder	Leek and celery soups	Braised celery and leeks; grilled meats; herrings; casseroles; salad dressings; stuffings	Biscuits; bread; scones
seed	Pickles	Cabbage; celery; curries; oily fish; pork; rabbit; stuffings; veal	None
NUTMEG	Cream soups	Fish; cabbage; chicken; egg and cheese dishes; meat loaves; pasta; pâtés; root vegetables	Biscuits; cakes; dried fruits; fruit salads; junkets; milk puddings; pastries; stewed fruits; sweet breads
OREGANO	Minestrone; pâtés; tomato soup	Egg dishes; green peppers; Italian dishes and pasta; onions; potatoes; quiches; stuffings	None
PAPRIKA	Dips; seafood; soups	Beef; curries; goulash; pork; pulses; rice; spiced meat dishes; veal; white fish	None
PARSLEY	All soups; fish and seafood	Baked and grilled fish; casseroles; egg and cheese dishes; herb butters; meats; most salads; pasta; sauces for poached fish; sautée dishes; vegetables	Savoury breads
PEPPER black	Clear soups; cream cheese dips; pickles	Most savoury dishes	Sweet cakes and biscuits
white	Cream soups; pickles; seafood	Casseroles; chicken; eggs; fish; mayonnaise; veal; white sauces	None
PEPPERCORNS, green	Cream cheese dips; seafood	All meat, poultry and game; herb butters; pâtés; sauces; sausages	With fresh strawberries
POPPY SEEDS	Dips; onion soup; spreads; sprinkled over chilled soups	Carrots; curries; peas; potatoes; salads; scattered over savoury pie crusts	Sprinkled over baked goods
ROSE	None	Rose petal vinegar for salads	Crystallised petals; rose hip syrup; rose hip tea; rose petal and hip wine; rose petal jam and jelly; rose petal tea; rose water
ROSEMARY	Chicken and tomato soups	Grills; lamb; pork; roasts; root vegetables; sautée dishes; some egg dishes; sparingly in salads	Flavour sugar; syrup for fruit salad
RUE	Cream and cottage cheese dips; egg spreads	Very sparingly in salads	None
SAFFRON	Soups (especially fish); cream cheese	Chicken; fish dishes; paella; pilaf and other savoury rice dishes; some egg dishes; turkey	Biscuits; bread; buns; cakes
SAGE	Cream and cottage cheese dips; tomato, celery, leek and lentil soups	Casseroles; cheese and egg dishes; herb butters; meat loaves; pâtés; pork; pulses; salads; sausages; stuffings for pork and poultry; veal	Herbal teas; savoury breads and scones
SALAD BURNET	Summer soups	Salads; stuffings; vinegar	None
SAVORY	Vegetable soups	Beef casseroles; broad and French beans; egg and cheese dishes; pork; pork pies and sausages; pulses; stuffings for pork and veal	None
SESAME SEEDS	In *hummus* (chick-pea dip); other dips	Dry-fried in salads; in salads; over vegetables *au gratin*, or fish and chicken dishes	Made into confectionery; scattered over bread, rolls, biscuits and pies
SORREL	Soup alone or with other vegetables	Egg dishes (especially omelettes); sauce for fish, chicken and veal; spinach; spring greens; stuffings for chicken, veal and lamb	Layer with brown sugar, raisins, and mixed spice to make sweet pie
STAR ANISE	Pickles	Chinese steamed fish; flavouring for Chinese boiled eggs; meats simmered in soy sauce	None
SWEET CICELY	Cream cheese dips	Green salads; omelettes; salad dressings	Fruit salads; pancakes
TANSY	Cream cheese dips	Beef casseroles; butters; omelettes and other egg dishes; stuffings	Apple pudding; flavour sugar
TARRAGON	Aspics; clear soups; tomato soups	Butters; carrots; chicken; fish; mushrooms; salads and dressings; some egg dishes; sauces; stuffings	Flavour sugar
THYME	Cream cheese; pâtés; vegetable and meat soups	Meat, lamb and chicken casseroles; meat loaves; pasta; stuffings; vegetables	Flavour sugar; herbal teas
TURMERIC	Curried and spiced soups; seafood	Curries; egg dishes; fish; rice	Colouring for bread and cakes
VANILLA POD	None	None	Custards and creams; drinks; ice-cream; milk puddings; sugar; wine cups
VIOLET	None	Vinegar for salads	Crystallised petals; white wine cups

Growing and Preserving Herbs

While bunches and sprigs of fresh herbs can be bought at supermarkets and green-grocers, for flavour and convenience, the best supply of herbs you can have is fresh ones that you have grown yourself. All the room you need is a small plot in the garden. If you haven't even this, you will find that herbs grow well in window boxes, in tubs on balconies and in pots indoors.

SITING THE HERB GARDEN

A herb garden should be as close as possible to the kitchen. If possible the plot should be south-facing, but if not, at least make sure that it is sheltered and catches as much sun as possible. Herbs like light, dry, well-drained soil. It does not have to be particularly rich, but if you can dig in some rotted manure or compost before you begin you will make growing conditions ideal. If the soil is rather acid, it is advisable to add lime to it.

LAYING OUT THE HERB GARDEN
Herbs are attractive plants and so it is easy to make the herb garden pretty as well as useful.

If the herbs are to grow in a border, make sure you know their full growing height and put the tallest at the back.

Some herbs, such as mint and lemon balm, spread rapidly. If you are growing them in an open bed it is best to control them so they do not take over. Knock the bottom from a bath, an old straight-sided sink, a tub or a large flower pot and sink it in the ground. Put the plants inside.

If you have plenty of room and a square or wide oblong plot, you can lay out your herbs in the fashion of an Elizabethan knot garden, where small, intricate patterns of different herbs were grown individually, surrounded by hedges of lavender, rosemary or low-growing box.

Another good idea is to make a chequerboard pattern with paving stones, so you have small, square beds of different herbs (see below). A chequerboard garden is easy to maintain and it helps to stop the larger herbs from spreading too much.

If you have only limited space you can still achieve an attractive pattern by growing your herbs within the spoke patterns of an old cart wheel (see below).

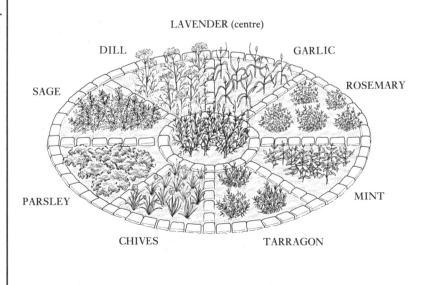

LAVENDER (centre)
DILL
GARLIC
SAGE
ROSEMARY
PARSLEY
MINT
CHIVES
TARRAGON

A variety of containers for growing herbs.

Of course, you do not have to set aside a special plot for herbs. They can be grown very successfully amongst vegetables and can even protect the vegetables from insect pests. Try growing sweet basil next to tomatoes, summer savory by broad beans; sage will protect carrots and thyme keeps away cabbage root fly.

In other parts of the garden herbs such as lavender and rosemary can make attractive, low hedges between flower beds. Bay trees can be decorative anywhere, whether in tubs or in open, sheltered ground. Chives make pretty edging plants, with their lilac-coloured flowers in summer.

CARING FOR THE HERB GARDEN
Herbs will give you little trouble and need the minimum of attention. Keep the ground weed-free, clear out and replant the annuals every year and cut back the perennials in autumn or spring. If possible, dig in a little well-rotted manure or compost every autumn or spring.

PROPAGATING HERBS
You can collect seed in the autumn from most annual plants and sow it in the prepared bed the following spring.

When perennial plants get old and woody, you can take cuttings from them or divide the roots. Make sure that your new plants are growing well before taking out the old ones.

GROWING HERBS IN TUBS
Herbs grown in tubs on balconies or patios can be made into an attractive feature. You can use wooden barrels cut in half and treated with wood preservative, stone tubs, or the largest flower pots that you can find. Mount the tubs on bricks and fill them where they are to stand, because they will be too heavy to carry.

Fill and plant the tubs in the spring. Put broken crockery or pieces of brick in the bottom, half fill the tubs with soil and shingle and top up with growing compost or soil.

Plant several herbs such as thyme, marjoram and parsley in one tub and make sure that they are watered regularly.

HERBS IN WINDOW-BOXES
What could be more convenient than a window-box of herbs growing outside the kitchen window? It is best if it is a window which gets plenty of sun and is sheltered from the strongest winds.

Make the box fit to the size of the window and make sure that you can reach it easily and open the window without the box falling off!

Put wire mesh in the bottom, then broken crockery or stones and top up with compost.

Water the plants whenever they look dry and cut them regularly.

GROWING HERBS INDOORS
Herbs thrive well if they are grown in small pots indoors. Parsley, chives, thyme, sage, rosemary and marjoram are most suitable, and basil will last longer indoors than out.

Choose 15-cm (6-inch) diameter pots and put them in a position where they will get plenty of light but will not get too hot. Water them regularly.

A charming Elizabethan custom was to grow herbs in hanging baskets, and these are useful when there is little space elsewhere. Make them in the spring. Line the baskets with moss and fill them with a mixture of good quality compost and soil.
They are best planted with low-growing, compact culinary herbs such as parsley, chives, thyme, marjoram and winter savory.

The baskets can be hung indoors or out. If putting them outside, hang them in the shed or greenhouse for a week first to harden them off. Make sure the baskets are watered regularly to prevent them drying out.

PRESERVING HERBS

It is a good idea to preserve all the herbs that you cannot pick during the winter. This will include all the annuals (e.g. chervil, basil) and those perennial plants that die right back such as lovage and fennel.

If you have large bushes of other perennials, such as thyme, sage and marjoram, you may not need to preserve them, but if your bushes are small and woody your winter supply of leaves will be sparse, so you will be wise to build up a winter store.

HARVESTING

Herbs contain volatile, or essential oils, which give the characteristic flavour and smell to different varieties. The content of these oils is greatest just before the herbs flower and at the start of the flowering period. It is at this time, therefore, that herbs should be cut for preserving.

Cut herbs on a dry, warm day, after the dew has dried but before the sun has become really hot. Handle them carefully and use good sharp scissors as bruising could cause loss of oils or discoloration.

You can safely take away about one third of perennial herbs such as sage and thyme. Try to shape the plants attractively as you do so. Annual plants such as sweet basil or summer savory can be cut to 7.5–10 cm (3–4 inches) from the ground. If you take out the centre spikes you will encourage the side shoots to grow thickly.

Cut only as many herbs as you can deal with in one day. Discard any blemished or discoloured twigs and take the herbs indoors and away from the sun immediately after cutting.

DRYING

Small quantities of herbs are best dried in bunches. Tie about ten sprigs together with strong thread

or fine cotton string. Hang them in a warm, dry, airy place, away from the light, such as in a well-ventilated attic, over a central heating boiler or in a not too hot airing cupboard. The temperature should not exceed 30°C (90°F).

Larger quantities of herbs are best dried on racks. These can be improvised by covering cake cooling racks with butter muslin or with brown paper into which you have punched holes with a skewer.

If you dry herbs frequently, make special stacking racks. Construct oblong frames of light wood, strengthened with diagonal cross pieces and with hessian or muslin stretched over them.

Stack the frames one above the other. These work best if they are all filled at once so the humidity remains the same. Put any new fresh herbs at the top as moisture rises.

Whether in bunches or on racks, most herbs will dry in 4 to 5 days. They should still be a bright, fresh colour and both twigs and leaves should snap crisply. If they are not completely dry, leave them a while longer, otherwise they may become musty.

DRYING HERBS IN A MICROWAVE OVEN

Finely chop the herbs and spread them out on a double layer of kitchen paper. Microwave on High for $1\frac{1}{2}$ minutes. Take them out and stir them about with your fingers to check if they are dry.

Delicate herbs, such as fresh coriander, will be dried after this time. Others need longer. Microwave on High again, checking and stirring after each minute. When done, the herbs will be dry, crisp and bright green.

DRYING HERB SEEDS

When the seeds are full but not quite brown, cut off the flower heads, together with about 15 cm (6 inches) of the stalk. Put the heads upside down in brown paper bags and hang them up to dry in the same way as bunches of herbs. After about 5 days, give the bags a shake and the seeds will drop down inside.

STORING DRIED HERBS

Strip the leaves carefully from the stems and leave them whole. This will preserve more flavour than crumbling them.

Dried herbs keep best in air-tight jars away from the light. Choose wood, earthenware or dark-coloured glass. See-through glass jars should be covered with paper or adhesive plastic covering.

In a cool larder, dried herbs will keep their flavour for 6–8 months. After that, any left can be scattered around the herb garden or sprinkled round pot plants to keep away insect pests.

USING DRIED HERBS

The flavour of dried herbs is very concentrated and consequently you will need much less than fresh herbs in any dish. Use the following equivalents:

Fresh	Dried
5 ml (1 tsp)	2.5 ml ($\frac{1}{2}$ tsp)
15 ml (1 tbsp)	5 ml (1 tsp)
45 ml (3 tbsp)	15 ml (1 tbsp)

Dried herbs tend to be tougher than fresh ones, so are best used in cooked dishes. If adding them to a salad, soak them for 30 minutes in the dressing first.

It is a good idea to keep some of your favourite dried herbs or herb mixtures in separate herb mills for ease of use.

You can also make your own bouquets garnis by tying small amounts of dried herb mixtures in circles of muslin.

FREEZING HERBS

Herbs with large fleshy leaves, such as basil, mint and parsley tend to freeze better than the delicate ones like fennel and dill. You can freeze herbs in polythene

bags, in ice cubes or chopped and spread out on trays. There is no need to blanch them first.

Whole leaves can be put in usable amounts in small polythene bags. Make sure they overlap as little as possible and freeze them flat. They can be chopped or crumbled and used when still frozen.

Sprigs of herbs can also be frozen in bags as can collections of sprigs tied together to make bouquets garnis. They can be taken straight from the freezer and popped into a casserole.

Cling-film may be used instead of bags but make sure it is sealed securely.

Pack the bags of frozen herbs, each type separately, in labelled boxes. The herbs will keep for up to 4 months.

To freeze herbs in ice cubes, finely chop them and pack them

into ice-cube trays so the compartments are two-thirds full. Top them up with cold water and open freeze them until solid. Take them out of the trays, then store them together in labelled polythene bags. These herb cubes can be added directly to sauces, soups, sautée dishes and casseroles. You can make them with single herbs or bouquet garnis mixtures.

To freeze herbs on trays, chop them and spread them out on the tray. Freeze them until they are hard and then pack them into tubs. They should stay loose and you can simply spoon them into whatever dish you are making. They are also suitable for adding to salads and sprinkling over foods before serving.

CANDYING FRUIT OR HERBS

SPICY CANDIED PEEL

| 6 oranges, lemons or grapefruit |
| 350 g (12 oz) granulated sugar |
| 5 whole cloves |

Wash or scrub the fruit thoroughly, halve or quarter it and remove the pulp. Simmer the peel in a little water for 1–2 hours until tender. (Change the water 2–3 times when cooking grapefruit peel.) Remove peel. Make the liquid up to 300 ml ($\frac{1}{2}$ pint) with water. Add 250 g (8 oz) of the sugar and the cloves, dissolve over a low heat, then bring to the boil. Add the peel, remove from the heat, cover and leave for 2 days.

Strain off the syrup, discarding the cloves. Dissolve another 100 g (4 oz) sugar in it and simmer the peel in this syrup until semi-transparent. The peel can be left in this thick syrup for 2–3 weeks. Drain off the syrup and place the peel on a wire rack to dry.

Put the rack in a warm place such as an airing cupboard, in the oven at the lowest setting with the door slightly ajar, or in the residual heat of the oven after cooking. The temperature should not exceed 50°C (120°F) or the fruit may brown and the flavour spoil. The drying will take several hours and is completed when the peel is no longer sticky. Store in airtight jars or containers.

CANDIED ANGELICA

| angelica shoots |
| salt |
| granulated sugar |

Drop the angelica shoots immediately into brine—7 g ($\frac{1}{4}$ oz) salt to 2.4 litres (4 pints) water—and leave for 10 minutes. Rinse in cold water. Boil the angelica for about 5 minutes until tender. Drain, retaining the liquid and scrape to remove the outer skin.

Using the angelica cooking liquid, make a syrup of 175 g (6 oz) sugar to 300 ml ($\frac{1}{2}$ pint) of the liquid. Place the angelica in a bowl, add the syrup, cover and leave for 24 hours. Drain off the syrup, add 50 g (2 oz) sugar to every 300 ml ($\frac{1}{2}$ pint) and bring to the boil. Pour back into the bowl over the angelica, cover and leave for 24 hours. Repeat this process a further five times until the syrup is of the consistency of runny honey. Boil the angelica for 2–3 minutes at the last addition of the sugar, then leave for 2 days. Dry off on a wire rack in a warm place or in the oven at 110°C (225°F) mark $\frac{1}{4}$. Store in screw-topped jars.

POT POURRIS

A bowl or jar of pot pourri will scent a room delicately and naturally. Pots pourris were first made in Elizabethan times to disguise the odour of old damp buildings. They were also believed to have curative properties, particularly where living conditions were insanitary. If you have fragrant flowers and herbs in the garden and are able to buy spices and essential oils, making a pot pourri should be easy.

There are four main types of ingredients in a pot pourri: those giving the predominant perfume; more subtly perfumed ones, to give an underlying scent; fixatives; and preservatives.

PREDOMINANT PERFUMES

These usually come mainly from sweet scented rose petals and lavender, but other strongly scented flowers and leaves can also be added. These include carnations, lilac, heliotrope, jonquil, jasmine, wallflower, magnolia and hyacinth. In the herb garden, find mints of all varieties: rosemary, woodruff, penny royal, pineapple sage and the many varieties of thyme, basil and lemon verbena. The scented leaves of geraniums and pelargoniums can also be added.

Strongly scented spices such as aniseed, coriander and fennel can be added to this mixture, together with the roots of ginger, sweet flag and angelica and dried orange and lemon peel.

UNDERLYING PERFUMES

These are added in smaller amounts to make a full-bodied scent. They come mainly from scented leaves such as thyme, marjoram, sage, bay, tansy, the scented geraniums, lemon balm and tarragon.

Sweet spices, either ground or whole, can also be added. These include cinnamon, nutmeg, allspice, cardamom and coriander.

Essential oils of herbs, which can be bought at chemists and herbalists, are further suggestions for improving the scent of a pot pourri. Add them only a drop at a time, stirring after each addition. They are very strong and too much would spoil the final result.

FIXATIVES

Adding a fixative will help to preserve the scent of a pot pourri. Dried, powdered orris root is the most common. Violet-scented, it is the root of *Iris germanica* and you can either grow and dry it yourself or buy it from herbalists.

Other plant fixatives include the dried powdered root of calamus (sweet flag); the dried pods of tonquin bean; the essential oil of sandalwood; and powdered resins such as gum benzoin and frankincense.

PRESERVATIVES

The preservatives prevent the ingredients of a pot pourri from decaying. Sea salt or another non-iodised salt is best for this purpose. Dry it in a low oven for several hours before use. Borax can also be used.

To keep the pot pourri dry, bury in it a small cotton bag of silica gel (available at chemists) which you can dry out occasionally in a low oven.

BASIC POT POURRI MIXTURE

1.5 litres (2¾ pints) predominant perfume mixture
450 ml (¾ pint) underlying perfume mixture
up to 3 drops strongly perfumed essential oil or up to 10 drops milder oil
fixative: 40 g (1½ oz) orris root or 75 g (3 oz) other
up to 300 ml (½ pint) preservative

DRY METHOD

Dry all the ingredients on racks as for herbs. As they dry, mix them with the appropriate amount of fixative and store them in airtight jars until you have enough to make up the mixture. Continue to dry herbs and flowers throughout the summer.

When all the flowers and herbs are dried and fixed, mix them with the preservative and a chosen mixture of spices, oils and a few pieces of citrus peels. Put them into a jar with a cotton bag containing about 100 g (4 oz) silica gel. Cover tightly and leave for 6–8 weeks. The pot pourri is then ready for use.

A mixture of dried flowers can be added to a dry-method pot pourri purely for their colour to add to the final appearance. These can include borage, delphinium, feverfew, heather, marigold, mullein, pansy and tansy.

MOIST METHOD

Making a pot pourri by the moist method preserves the scent for a longer time, but the colour will not be as good.

Half dry the petals and leaves until they have a leathery texture. Then mix them together and layer them in a large jar with half their volume of preservative. If this does not fill the jar, more can be added over a period of 3 days. Stir before adding more layers. When the jar is full, cover tightly and leave it in a dark place for 2 weeks.

Take out the solid mass which has formed and break it up. Add fixative and oils as required, a drop at a time.

KEEPING THE POT POURRI

If a pot pourri is kept in an open bowl it will perfume the room strongly for a few weeks but after that will lose its scent. It is best kept in a closed container and uncovered and stirred periodically. 'Refresher oils' are available. Use these from time to time.

Choose glass containers for pot pourri made by the dry method, and earthenware or pottery for that made by the moist method.

HERBAL RINSES

Dried rosemary makes a refreshing hair rinse for mousey to dark hair; dried chamomile brings out the highlights of fair hair. It's best to make several rinse sachets at a time, storing them in any attractive jar that has an air-tight lid.

Make some sachets by cutting 5-cm (2-inch) squares of muslin or cheesecloth. Put a teaspoonful of dried rosemary or chamomile in the centre of each square, and tie the squares into a bundle with a piece of cotton. When you need a hair rinse, place one of the sachets in 600 ml (1 pint) of already boiling water, remove from the heat, and leave to cool.

MAKING A SCENTED BATH BAG

These little lavender bags are meant for hanging on a ribbon from a bath tap, so the hot water flows through them and becomes permeated with fragrance. Of course, you can use other ingredients if you want a different scent — perhaps a mixture of orange blossom, lime blossom and eau de cologne mint — but really anything with a good smell will fit the bill.

The bags themselves are very easy to make. Cut two small squares from scraps of tiny-printed fabric, using pinking shears to give a decorative edge. Stitch wrong sides together along three sides.

Buy a 70-cm (28-inch) length of narrow ribbon, and about 1.5 cm ($\frac{5}{8}$ inch) down from the top of the bag, stitch the ribbon to both sides of the bag, about 13 cm (5 inch) in from each end of ribbon.

Fill the bag with dried lavender, then tie the 13-cm (5-inch) ribbon-ends tightly to one side of the bag with a single knot. This will close the neck of the bag securely. Then tie the ribbon-ends to the other side and finish with a bow. The central portion of ribbon will form a loop for tap-hanging.

MAKING A POMANDER

The original pomander of Elizabethan times consisted of a strongly scented pot pourri, formed into a ball with fragrant gum or wax and worn round the neck or waist in a small, perforated container. It was thought to ward off diseases.

Another type, more frequently carried by doctors and court officials, consisted of an orange or lemon stuck with cloves. This orange pomander is easy to make. It can be hung in the wardrobe, put into a linen drawer or, alternatively, placed in a pot pourri jar.

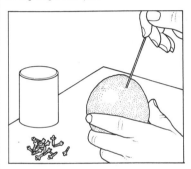

Choose a small, thin-skinned orange, free from blemishes. Prick holes in the peel with a darning needle or fine skewer, leaving a cross pattern round

which you will eventually tie a ribbon. Make the holes fairly close together, and do not go so deep as to let the juice run out.

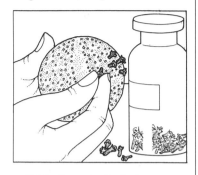

Stick cloves in the holes so the spaces between the cross are covered completely. Mix equal parts of ground cinnamon and orris root. Roll the orange in the mixture, rubbing and patting the powder well in. A little freshly grated nutmeg and ground ginger may also be added.

Wrap the orange in grease-proof paper or put it into a brown paper bag. Leave it in a cool, dark place for 5–6 weeks or until it is hard and dry. Shake off any loose powder and tie the pomander round with ribbon. It should keep its scent for several years.

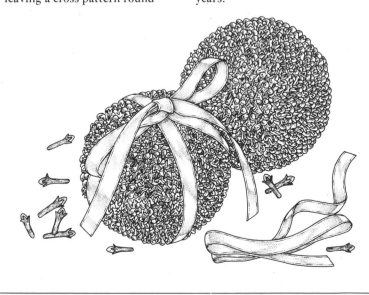

Cooking with Herbs and Spices

Herbs and spices are very versatile and complement a wide variety of ingredients. In this chapter you will see that as well as being essential in many sauces and stuffings, they can be used to flavour all kinds of everyday and special occasion dishes.

HERB BUTTERS

Herb butter is made by beating finely chopped herbs into softened, unsalted butter. Other ingredients may also be added, such as grated orange or lemon rind, crushed garlic, a squeeze of lemon juice, crushed green peppercorns, ground black pepper and salt.

The finished butter may be used as it is for tossing with cooked vegetables or, if it is not too strongly flavoured, for spreading on bread or canapés. Most often, it is formed into a roll, wrapped in foil or greaseproof paper and chilled until it is firm. It is then cut into slices and used to top grilled meats or plainly cooked fish.

PARSLEY BUTTER (MAÎTRE D'HÔTEL)

100 g (4 oz) butter
30 ml (2 tbsp) finely chopped fresh parsley
good squeeze of lemon juice
salt
cayenne pepper

1 Cream the butter until soft. Add to it the remaining ingredients and beat together.

2 Shape the butter into a roll and wrap it in greaseproof paper or kitchen foil. Leave in the refrigerator to harden.

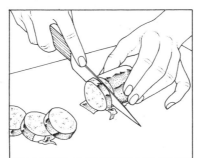

3 To serve, cut into pats about 5 mm ($\frac{1}{4}$ in) thick. Serve with grilled fish, steak or egg dishes.

HERB LOAF

Heat the oven to 200°C (400°F) mark 6. Cut a white or wholewheat French loaf into thick diagonal slices. Spread 100 g (4 oz) herb butter and reshape the loaf. Sprinkle it lightly with water and wrap it in aluminium foil. Bake in the oven at 180°C (350°F) mark 4 for 15 minutes.

CINNAMON BUTTER

50 g (2 oz) unsalted butter
50 g (2 oz) caster sugar
10 ml (2 tsp) ground cinnamon

Cream together all the ingredients until blended. Use as a spread on hot toast or warm scones.

GHEE

Ghee is a form of clarified butter used in Asian cookery.

225 g (8 oz) butter

1 Melt the butter in a heavy saucepan over medium heat. Simmer until a thick froth forms on top.

2 Reduce the heat and let the butter simmer gently until the froth starts to separate from the clear butter and some of the sediment settles at the bottom.

3 Simmer for one more minute making sure the butter does not burn. Remove the pan from the heat. Cool the butter slightly.

4 Line a metal sieve with muslin, a thin tea towel or a double layer of kitchen paper. Strain the butter into a glass storage jar or other non-plastic container. Discard the sediment left in the bottom of the pan.

5 Let the ghee cool and set and cover it tightly with cling-film. Keeps indefinitely if refrigerated.

HERB CHEESES

Herbs have been used in the making of cheeses for centuries, both to flavour and to act as a co-agulant instead of rennet.

Most often, mixtures of herbs and often garlic are beaten into soft cream and medium fat cheeses. You can buy these ready made or devise your own favourite herb mixtures. Finely chopped red and green peppers or crushed black or green peppercorns can also be added.

Herbs and spices such as mace can also be added to potted cheese.

POTTED CHEESE WITH HERBS

225 g (8 oz) semi-hard cheese such as Cheshire

60 ml (4 tbsp) chopped mixed parsley, thyme, sage, savory, chives and tarragon

90 ml (6 tbsp) bitter beer

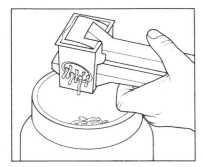

1 Grate the cheese into a double saucepan and mix in the herbs and beer. Set the pan on a low heat and stir until the mixture is creamy and blended together.

2 Pour the cheese either into four small pots or into an earthenware bowl. Chill until firm. Serve with oatcakes and apples.

GOAT'S CHEESE IN OIL

4 small rindless goat's cheeses (sometimes called Crottin)

1 sprig rosemary

1 sprig thyme

2 garlic cloves, skinned

1 bay leaf

12 black peppercorns

450–600 ml ($\frac{3}{4}$–1 pint) olive oil

1 Pack the cheese in a jar and add the herbs and pepper-corns. Cover with the oil and seal.

2 Leave for 2–3 weeks before using and eat within 6–8 weeks.

3 Serve on toast or French bread that has been sprinkled with a little oil from the jar. Use any remaining oil for French dressing.

PEPPER AND HERB CREAM CHEESE

568 ml (1 pint) single cream

568 ml (1 pint) milk

30 ml (2 tbsp) buttermilk

15 ml (1 tbsp) chopped mixed parsley, chervil and thyme

5 ml (1 tsp) salt

30 ml (2 tbsp) coarsely crushed black peppercorns

1 Put the cream and milk into a saucepan and warm them gently to blood heat or 32–38°C (90–100°F). Stir in the butter-milk. Pour the mixture into a bowl.

2 Cover the bowl with cling film and leave it in a warm place for 24–48 hours or until the cream mixture turns to soft curds.

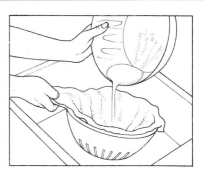

3 Line a colander with muslin and place it in the sink. Pour the curds into the colander and drain for 10 minutes. Place the colander on a rack over a large bowl. Cover with cling film and chill for a further 18–24 hours.

4 Spoon the curds from the col-ander into a bowl and stir in the mixed herbs and salt. Pour off the whey from the saucepan.

5 Line a small plastic punnet pierced with small holes or earthenware cheese mould with a double layer of damp cheesecloth, leaving a 5 cm (2 inch) overhang. Spoon in the curds and fold the cheesecloth over the top.

6 Place the cheese on a wire rack in a baking tin. Cover it tightly with cling film and chill for 18–24 hours.

7 To serve, unmould the cheese onto a plate, discard the cheesecloth and press the pepper over the cheese.

——————— VARIATION ———————

GARLIC AND CHIVE DIP

Mix together **100 g (4 oz) full fat soft cheese** and **30 ml (2 tbsp) single cream** thoroughly. Add **1 garlic clove, crushed to a paste**, **30 ml (2 tbsp) chopped chives**, **10 ml (2 tsp) lemon juice** and **salt and freshly ground pepper** and mix well. Chill for at least 2 hours before serving.

SAUCES AND DRESSINGS

MINT SAUCE

Makes about 150 ml (5 fl oz)

25 g (1 oz) mint leaves
45 ml (3 tbsp) boiling water
15 ml (3 tsp) sugar
60 ml (4 tbsp) white wine vinegar

Finely chop the mint leaves and put them into a small jug. Pour on the boiling water and leave them for 10 minutes. Stir in the sugar and then the vinegar.

Serve with roast lamb.

MUSTARD SAUCE

Makes 300 ml ($\frac{1}{2}$ pint)

50 g (2 oz) butter
15 ml (1 tbsp) flour
300 ml ($\frac{1}{2}$ pint) boiling water
salt and freshly ground white pepper
10 ml (2 tsp) lemon juice, or more to taste
5 ml (1 tsp) English mustard, or 10 ml (2 tsp) French or Dijon mustard
1 egg yolk (optional)

1 Melt 15 g ($\frac{1}{2}$ oz) butter in a saucepan. Stir in the flour. When smooth, pour in all the boiling water, stirring briskly all the time.

2 Add the remaining butter in small pieces, beating it in well. Season and add the lemon juice and mustard and beat well. For a richer sauce, beat in the egg yolk.

CAPER SAUCE

Make as for mustard sauce, substituting **30 ml (2 tbsp) chopped capers** and **15 ml (1 tbsp) chopped fresh parsley** for the **mustard**.

PESTO

Makes about 300 ml ($\frac{1}{2}$ pint)

50 g (2 oz) fresh basil leaves
2 garlic cloves, skinned
30 ml (2 tbsp) pine nuts
salt and freshly ground black pepper
50 g (2 oz) freshly grated Parmesan cheese
100 ml (4 fl oz) olive oil
30 ml (2 tbsp) double cream

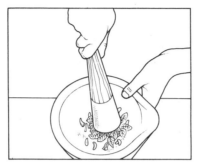

1 Put the basil, garlic, pine nuts, salt and pepper into a mortar and grind until a paste is formed.

2 Add the cheese and blend well. Transfer to a bowl and beat in the oil, a little at a time, stirring vigorously with a wooden spoon. When all the oil has been added, fold in the cream. Serve cold, with freshly cooked pasta.

--- VARIATION ---

To make in a blender or food processor, place the basil, garlic, pine nuts, seasoning and olive oil in the blender or food processor and blend at high speed until very creamy. Transfer the mixture to a bowl, fold in the cheese and cream and mix thoroughly.

Store the sauce for up to 2 weeks in a screw-topped jar in the refrigerator.

VINAIGRETTE (FRENCH DRESSING)

Makes about 125 ml (4 fl oz) dressing

90 ml (6 tbsp) olive or vegetable oil
30 ml (2 tbsp) wine, cider or herb vinegar
2.5 ml ($\frac{1}{2}$ tsp) sugar
2.5 ml ($\frac{1}{2}$ tsp) mustard (e.g. wholegrain, Dijon, French or mustard powder)
salt and freshly ground black pepper

Place the ingredients in a bowl or screw-topped jar and whisk or shake together until well blended. The oil separates out on standing, so whisk or shake again before use.

● If a recipe calls for 150 ml ($\frac{1}{4}$ pint) dressing, add an extra 15 ml (1 tbsp) oil.

● The dressing can be stored in a bottle or screw-topped jar for several months in the refrigerator.

--- VARIATIONS ---

FRESH HERB VINAIGRETTE

Add **15 ml (1 tbsp) chopped fresh parsley**, **15 ml (1 tbsp) chopped fresh mint** or **10 ml (2 tsp) chopped chives** or a mixture of all three.

CURRY VINAIGRETTE

Add **5 ml (1 tsp) curry powder** to the basic vinaigrette.

DILL CREAM DRESSING

142 ml (5 fl oz) soured cream
2.5 ml ($\frac{1}{2}$ tsp) onion salt
30 ml (2 tbsp) chopped fresh parsley
15 ml (1 tbsp) chopped fresh dill
salt and freshly ground black pepper

Put all the ingredients into a bowl and mix well together. Allow to infuse for at least 15 minutes.

Serve as a dressing for coleslaw or cucumber salads.

MAYONNAISE

Makes about 300 ml (½ pint)

2 egg yolks
1 tsp mustard powder
salt
freshly ground white pepper
300 ml (½ pint) olive or vegetable oil
30 ml (2 tbsp) white wine vinegar

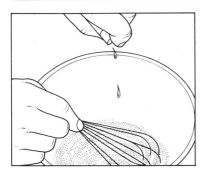

Put the egg yolks into a bowl. Beat in the mustard powder and seasonings. Beat in 30 ml (2 tbsp) oil, drop by drop and beating after each addition. Beat in 10 ml (2 tsp) vinegar. Gradually beat in remaining oil so mixture becomes very thick. Add remaining vinegar to taste.

——— VARIATIONS ———

CAPER MAYONNAISE
Add **10 ml (2 tsp) chopped capers**, **5 ml (1 tsp) chopped red pepper** and **2.5 ml (½ tsp) tarragon vinegar**. Serve as an accompaniment to fish.

CURRY MAYONNAISE
Add **5 ml (1 tsp) curry powder** to the yolks before adding the oil.

RÉMOULADE SAUCE
To the basic mayonnaise, add **15 ml (1 tbsp) each chopped gherkins and capers, 15 ml (1 tbsp) mixed chopped parsley, chervil and tarragon and 2 chopped anchovy fillets**.

GREEN GODDESS DRESSING

Makes about 300 ml (½ pint)

150 ml (¼ pint) mayonnaise
142 ml (5 fl oz) soured cream
30 ml (2 tbsp) chopped fresh parsley
30 ml (2 tbsp) chopped fresh chives
4 anchovy fillets, finely chopped
30 ml (2 tbsp) cider vinegar
salt and freshly ground black pepper

Mix all the ingredients together, seasoning well. Allow to stand for several hours before use.

Store for up to 4 days in a screw-topped jar in the refrigerator.

AÏOLI

Makes about 300 ml (½ pint)

4 garlic cloves, skinned
1.25 ml (¼ tsp) salt
2 egg yolks
300 ml (½ pint) olive oil
30 ml (2 tbsp) lemon juice

1 Crush the garlic cloves to a smooth paste with a little salt. Place in a mortar or bowl. Add the yolks and remaining salt; beat well with a pestle or spoon. Gradually beat in the oil, a drop at a time, until mixture is thick and smooth.

2 When all oil is added, add remaining lemon juice to taste. Store for up to 4 days in a screw-topped jar in the refrigerator.

TARTARE SAUCE

Makes about 300 ml (½ pint)

2 hard-boiled egg yolks
1 raw egg yolk
salt and freshly ground white pepper
300 ml (½ pint) olive oil
30 ml (2 tbsp) white wine vinegar
15 ml (1 tbsp) chopped fresh parsley
10 ml (2 tsp) chopped fresh chives
10 ml (2 tsp) chopped capers or gherkins

Sieve the hard-boiled egg yolks into a bowl. Add the raw yolk and seasonings and work them together well. Add the oil, drop by drop, as for mayonnaise. Add the vinegar to taste and mix in the herbs and capers or gherkins.

BÉCHAMEL SAUCE

Makes 300 ml (½ pint)

300 ml (½ pint) milk
1 slice onion
1 bay leaf
6 black peppercorns
1 blade mace
20 g (¾ oz) butter
20 ml (4 tsp) flour
salt and freshly ground white pepper

1 Put the milk into a saucepan with the onion slice, bay leaf, peppercorns and mace. Set it on a gentle heat for 5 minutes. Strain it and rinse the saucepan.

2 Melt the butter in the pan. Stir in the flour and cook gently, for 1 minute, stirring. Remove pan from the heat and gradually stir in the milk. Bring to the boil, stirring and cook for 1–2 minutes until thick. Season.

——— VARIATION ———

PARSLEY SAUCE
Add **50 g (2 oz) finely chopped parsley** to the béchamel sauce for the 2 minutes simmering time.

BÉARNAISE SAUCE

Makes about 150 ml (5 fl oz)

45 ml (3 tbsp) white wine vinegar
6 black peppercorns
$\frac{1}{2}$ bay leaf
1 blade mace
1 slice onion
2 tarragon leaves
2 egg yolks
salt and freshly ground pepper
100 g ($3\frac{1}{2}$ oz) unsalted butter
10 ml (2 tsp) glaze or jelly at base of beef dripping (optional)
5 ml (1 tsp) mixed chopped tarragon, parsley and chervil
5 ml (1 tsp) snipped fresh chives

1 Put the vinegar, peppercorns, bay leaf, mace, onion and tarragon leaves into a small saucepan. Bring the vinegar to the boil and boil until it is reduced to 15 ml (1 tbsp). Remove from the heat.

2 Cream the egg yolks in a bowl with 15 g ($\frac{1}{2}$ oz) butter and a pinch of salt. Strain in the vinegar and beat well.

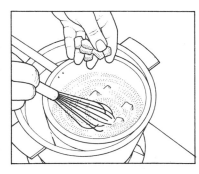

3 Put the bowl into a saucepan of boiling water and turn off the heat. Stir until the mixture begins to thicken. Beat in the butter in small pieces. Beat in the meat glaze if using. Season to taste and add the herbs. Serve warm.

HOLLANDAISE SAUCE

Makes about 150 ml ($\frac{1}{4}$ pint)

60 ml (4 tbsp) white wine vinegar
6 black peppercorns
1 blade mace
1 slice onion
1 bay leaf
3 egg yolks
150 g (5 oz) unsalted butter
salt and freshly ground pepper
10 ml (2 tsp) lemon juice
30 ml (2 tbsp) single cream

1 Put the vinegar into a small saucepan with the peppercorns, mace, onion and bay leaf. Boil to reduce to 15 ml (1 tbsp). Set aside.

2 Beat the egg yolks in a bowl with 15 g ($\frac{1}{2}$ oz) butter and a pinch of salt. Strain in the vinegar. Put the bowl into a saucepan of boiling water. Turn off the heat and beat in the remaining butter, in small pieces. Beat until thick. Remove from pan. Season to taste and beat in lemon juice and cream. Serve immediately.

HORSERADISH SAUCE

Makes about 225 ml (8 fl oz)

75 g (3 oz) grated horseradish
5 ml (1 tsp) mustard powder
5 ml (1 tsp) sugar
10 ml (2 tsp) white wine vinegar
150 ml (5 fl oz) double cream, lightly whipped

Mix all the ingredients together and leave the sauce to stand for 20 minutes before serving.

FLAVOURED SALT AND SUGAR

Herb or spice salts can be added to salad dressings and soups. Use them to season vegetables and to rub sparingly over meat before roasting or grilling.

Herb sugars are delicious in custards or sweet soufflés, or sprinkled onto cakes, biscuits or sweet pastries. Suitable herbs include rosemary, thyme and lemon thyme, angelica, sweet cicely, marjoram and scented geraniums. Peppermint and lemon balm sugars are delicious sprinkled over fruit salads.

To make herb sugar: put a sprig of the fresh herb into a jar of caster sugar. Seal it and leave the herb to scent and flavour the sugar for about three weeks. It can be left in the jar while the sugar is in use. For a continual supply of herb sugar, the jar can be topped up with more sugar and the old sprig replaced with a fresh one.

VANILLA SUGAR
Make as herb sugar, using a vanilla pod instead of fresh herbs.

CINNAMON SUGAR
Make as vanilla sugar, using a cinnamon stick instead of the vanilla pod.

HERB SALTS
To make a herb salt: mix **equal volume** of the chosen **herbs** and **non-iodised salt**. Spread the mixture on a baking sheet and put it in a very low oven with the door left slightly ajar for 30 minutes. (The warmth releases essential oils of the herbs which are absorbed by the salt). Cool and store in a screw-topped jar.

SPICED SALTS
Spiced salt is used in the same ways as herb salt. Pound **non-iodised salt** with equal quantities of spices such as **cumin, celery** or **fennel** seeds or **allspice** and **juniper** berries.

STUFFINGS

THYME STUFFING

Makes about 200 g (7 oz)

50 g (2 oz) butter

1 small onion, skinned and finely chopped

75 g (3 oz) fresh white or wholemeal breadcrumbs

15 ml (1 tbsp) chopped fresh thyme

15 ml (1 tbsp) chopped fresh parsley

10 ml (2 tsp) chopped fresh marjoram

finely grated rind and juice of 1 lemon

1 egg, beaten

salt and freshly ground pepper

Melt the butter in a frying pan on a low heat. Add the onion and fry for 5 minutes until soft. Remove the pan from the heat and stir in the remaining ingredients.
    Use for stuffing lamb or poultry.

MINT AND ROSEMARY STUFFING

Enough stuffing for one end of a 4.5–5.4 kg (10–12 lb) turkey

225 g (8 oz) onions

2 celery sticks

225 g (8 oz) fresh white or wholemeal breadcrumbs

30 ml (2 tbsp) mint sauce (page 150)

10 ml (2 tsp) chopped fresh rosemary

finely grated rind of 1 lemon

salt and freshly ground pepper

1 egg, beaten

Finely chop the onion and celery and soften them in the butter. In a large bowl, mix together the breadcrumbs, mint sauce, rosemary and lemon rind. Stir in the celery and onion. Mix well and bind together with the egg.

LEMON BALM STUFFING

Makes about 450 g (1 lb)

225 g (8 oz) dried prunes

225 g (8 oz) cooking apples

15 g ($\frac{1}{2}$ oz) fresh lemon balm leaves, finely chopped

1 egg yolk

Stone and chop the prunes. Peel, core and chop the apples. Mix them with the lemon balm leaves and bind the mixture with the egg yolk. Use for stuffing duck.

SAGE AND ONION STUFFING

Makes about 400 g (14 oz)

2 large onions, skinned and chopped

15 g ($\frac{1}{2}$ oz) butter, melted

100 g (4 oz) fresh white or wholemeal breadcrumbs

30 ml (2 tbsp) chopped fresh sage or 10 ml (2 tsp) dried sage

salt and freshly ground pepper

Put the onions in a saucepan of cold water. Bring to the boil and simmer them until tender, about 10 minutes. Drain well and mix with the remaining ingredients. Use for stuffing pork or poultry.

PARSLEY STUFFING

Makes about 225 g (8 oz)

25 g (1 oz) butter

1 onion, finely chopped

75 g (3 oz) fresh white or wholemeal breadcrumbs

60 ml (4 tbsp) chopped parsley

finely grated rind of 1 lemon

juice of $\frac{1}{2}$ lemon

60 ml (4 tbsp) dry white wine

Melt the butter in a frying pan, add the onion and fry gently for 5 minutes until soft. Take pan from heat and mix in remaining ingredients. Use for stuffing poultry.

SPICY APRICOT STUFFING

Makes about 175 g (6 oz)

75 g (3 oz) dried apricots

75 g (3 oz) fresh breadcrumbs

1.25 ml ($\frac{1}{4}$ tsp) ground mixed spice

15 ml (1 tbsp) chopped fresh parsley

salt and black pepper

15 ml (1 tbsp) lemon juice

25 g (1 oz) butter, melted

1 egg, size 6, beaten

Soak the apricots overnight in cold water. Drain and chop them. Mix them with all the remaining ingredients. Use for stuffing pork, lamb or chicken.

APRICOT-CURRY STUFFING

Makes about 450 g (16 oz)

175 g (6 oz) fresh breadcrumbs

100 g (4 oz) dried apricots, finely chopped

15 ml (1 tbsp) chopped fresh parsley

50 g (2 oz) butter

100 g (4 oz) onion, skinned and finely chopped

juice and grated rind of 1 orange

7.25 ml (1$\frac{1}{2}$ level tsp) curry powder

salt and pepper

1 egg, size 6, beaten

1 Place the breadcrumbs in a bowl and add the apricots and parsley. Melt the butter in a small saucepan, add the onion and orange rind; cook until soft.

2 Remove from the pan and add to the breadcrumbs. Sprinkle in the curry powder and cook gently for 1 minute. Pour 45 ml (3 tbsps) orange juice over and bubble gently for 30 seconds.

3 Blend the curried orange juice into the breadcrumbs. Season and bind with egg.

FLAVOURED VINEGARS AND OILS

Herb and spice vinegars and oils will give a subtle flavour to dressings, marinades and sauces.

MAKING HERB OIL

Herb oils can also be brushed over meat and fish before grilling. To make a herb oil, choose a bland oil such as sunflower, groundnut or safflower oil, or a mild olive oil.

Most culinary herbs are suitable. Choose from rosemary, thyme, tarragon, marjoram, fennel, savory, sage and basil. They should all be used fresh. Lightly bruise enough herb sprigs to half-fill a glass bottle or jar. Cover them with oil and seal with non-corrosive tops.

Leave the oil for 2 weeks in a warm place. Shake once a day.

Strain the oil, pressing down hard on the herbs. Taste. If the flavour is not strong enough, repeat the process. When the oil is ready, decant into bottles and seal.

MAKING HERB VINEGAR

A good-quality white or red wine vinegar is the best for making most herb vinegars. Most fresh herbs can be used as a flavouring (never use dried ones).

Chop enough fresh herbs to half fill a bottle. Warm double their volume of wine vinegar and pour it over the herbs. Cover tightly

and leave in a cool, dry place for about 6 weeks.

Strain the vinegar through muslin. Taste and add more vinegar if the flavour is too strong. Pour into bottles and seal with air-tight, corrosion-proof tops.

CHILLI VINEGAR

Make as for Herb Vinegar, using **25 g (1 oz) crushed, dried red chillies** to every **600 ml (1 pint) wine vinegar** instead of herbs.

GARLIC VINEGAR

3 garlic cloves, skinned and coarsely chopped
600 ml (1 pint) distilled malt vinegar

1 Place the garlic in a warmed jar. Bring the vinegar to the boil and pour it onto the garlic.

2 Allow to cool and cover with a non-corrosive seal. Leave in a cool place for 1 week. Taste.

3 If the flavour is strong enough, strain the vinegar and bottle. If you prefer a stronger flavour, leave vinegar for a few days more.

HORSERADISH VINEGAR

Make as for Herb Vinegar, using **40 g (1½ oz) grated fresh horseradish** to every **600 ml (1 pint) wine vinegar** instead of herbs.

SPICED VINEGAR FOR PICKLES

1.2 litres (2 pints) distilled malt vinegar
15 g (½ oz) white mustard seeds
2.5 ml (½ tsp) black peppercorns
5 ml (1 tsp) cloves
5 ml (1 tsp) allspice berries
4 dried red chillies
1 piece cinnamon stick or cassia bark

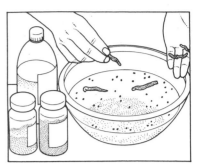

1 Put the vinegar and spices in a large bowl or earthenware casserole. Cover tightly.

2 Stand container in a saucepan of water. Bring water to boil and remove from heat. Leave container in pan for 2 hours. Strain. Use immediately or bottle tightly.

CHILLI OIL

The use of chilli oil will give an underlying hot flavour. Bottled chilli oil can be bought in oriental stores, but to make it yourself, bruise six dried red chillies, put them into a jar with 600 ml (1 pint) sunflower or groundnut oil and leave them to infuse on a sunny windowsill for 2–3 weeks. It will keep indefinitely.

HARISSA (FIERY SAUCE)

25 g (1 oz) dried red chillies
1 garlic clove, skinned and chopped
5 ml (1 tsp) caraway seed
5 ml (1 tsp) cumin seed
5 ml (1 tsp) coriander seed
pinch of salt
olive oil

1 Soak chillies in hot water for 1 hour. Drain well, then grind into a paste in a pestle and mortar or in an electric mill together with the garlic clove and spices. Add a pinch of salt.

2 Put into a jar, cover with olive oil and seal. It will keep in the refrigerator for up to 2 months. The oil can be used in salad dressings.

JELLIES AND RELISHES

Herb jellies are traditionally served with roast meats. Rosemary or mint will go with roast lamb; parsley with gammon; sage with pork; and thyme with poultry.

HERB JELLY

2.5 kg (5 lb) cooking apples
1.2 litres (2 pints) water
few sprigs of chosen fresh herb
1.2 litres (2 pints) distilled vinegar
sugar
90–120 ml (6–8 tbsp) chopped fresh mint, parsley or thyme; or 90 ml (6 tbsp) chopped fresh sage; or 60 ml (4 tbsp) chopped fresh rosemary

1 Remove any bruised or damaged parts from the apples. Roughly chop them without peeling or coring.

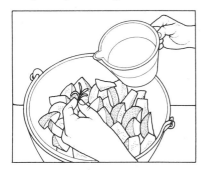

2 Put them into a large saucepan with the water and herb sprigs. Bring to the boil and simmer gently for 4–5 minutes or until soft and pulpy, stirring from time to time to prevent sticking. Add the vinegar and boil for a further 5 minutes.

3 Spoon the apple pulp into a jelly bag and leave it to strain into a large bowl for at least 12 hours.

4 Discard the pulp. Measure the liquid and put it into a preserving pan with 500 g (1 lb) sugar for each 600 ml (1 pint) liquid. Heat gently, stirring, until the sugar has dissolved. Boil rapidly for 10 minutes.

5 Test for setting. When the setting point is reached, take the pan from the heat and remove any scum with a slotted spoon. Stir in the chopped herbs.
    Cool slightly. Stir again to distribute the herb. Pot and cover in the usual way.

SWEET CIDER JELLY

Makes about 2.75 kg (5½ lb)

1.2 litres (2 pints) sweet apple cider
thinly pared rind 2 oranges
15 ml (1 tbsp) chopped fresh rosemary
1.4 kg (3 lb) sugar
1 bottle liquid pectin

Put the cider, orange rind and rosemary into a large saucepan. Bring slowly to the boil and reduce the heat. Add the sugar and stir to dissolve it, without boiling. Add the pectin and bring to a fast rolling boil. Boil hard for 1 minute. Strain into warm pots and cover.
    Serve with pork and bacon roasts.

APPLE AND MINT RELISH

275 g (10 oz) cooking apples
150 ml (5 fl oz) natural yogurt
30 ml (2 tbsp) chopped fresh mint
salt and freshly ground black pepper

Peel and coarsely grate the apple. Stir it into the yogurt together with the mint and seasoning.
    Spoon into a serving dish. Cover with cling film and chill for 30 minutes before serving.
    Serve with roast meats.

MUSTARDS

HONEY MUSTARD

Makes about 60 ml (4 tbsp)

30 ml (2 tbsp) mustard powder
5 ml (1 tsp) honey
30 ml (2 tbsp) dry white wine or cider
warm water (optional)

Put the mustard into a pot. Add the honey and wine or cider and mix well. Add warm water if needed for right consistency.

TARRAGON MUSTARD

Makes about 45 ml (3 tbsp)

30 ml (2 tbsp) mustard powder
10 ml (2 tsp) chopped tarragon
15 ml (1 tbsp) tarragon vinegar
warm water

Put the mustard powder and tarragon into a bowl. Mix in vinegar and then enough warm water to make it the right consistency.

WHOLEGRAIN MUSTARD

Makes about 120 ml (8 tbsp)

50 g (2 oz) black mustard seeds
50 g (2 oz) white mustard seeds
2.5 ml (½ tsp) salt
1.25 ml (¼ tsp) freshly ground black pepper
30 ml (2 tbsp) dark soft brown Barbados sugar
cider vinegar or herb vinegar

1 Put the mustards, salt, pepper and sugar into a bowl. Just cover them with the vinegar. Leave them for 24 hours.

2 Lightly blend in an electric blender or food processor. As the mixture thickens in the blender you may need to add more vinegar or, if cider vinegar has been used, dry cider. Put into a jar and cover with a non-corrosive lid.

HERB AND SPICE MIXTURES

BOUQUET GARNI

A bouquet garni is the French term for a small bunch of herbs and spices which is used to add flavour to stews, casseroles, soups etc. Bouquets garnis can be bought ready made, though the flavour of a freshly made bouquet is far superior.

For the basic bouquet garni, tie together 2 sprigs parsley, 1 of thyme and 1 bay leaf.

If using dried herbs, tie together in a muslin bag 5 ml (1 tsp) dried parsley, 2.5 ml ($\frac{1}{2}$ tsp) dried thyme and $\frac{1}{2}$ bay leaf, crumbled.

● If liked, 1 sprig of fresh marjoram can be added with the thyme; or 2.5 ml ($\frac{1}{2}$ tsp) dried.

● To go with lamb, add 1 rosemary sprig to the basic bunch of fresh herbs; 1.25 ml ($\frac{1}{4}$ tsp) dried crumbled rosemary to muslin bag.

● To go with pork, add 1 sprig each of sage and savory; or 1.25 ml ($\frac{1}{4}$ tsp) each of dried.

● To go with beef, add 1 thinly pared strip orange rind and 1 sprig of celery leaves; or 1.25 ml ($\frac{1}{4}$ tsp) dried grated orange rind.

● To go with chicken, use lemon thyme instead of thyme and tie in 1 strip lemon rind; or add 2.5 ml ($\frac{1}{2}$ tsp) dried lemon thyme.

● To go with fish, replace the thyme with lemon thyme and add a sprig of fresh fennel; or add 2.5 ml ($\frac{1}{2}$ tsp) dried lemon thyme and 1.25 ml ($\frac{1}{4}$ tsp) dried fennel.

FINES HERBES

25 g (1 oz) chopped fresh parsley
15 g ($\frac{1}{2}$ oz) chopped fresh chervil
15 g ($\frac{1}{2}$ oz) chopped fresh chives
30 ml (2 tbsp) chopped fresh tarragon

Mix the herbs together and use to flavour omelettes and other egg dishes, fish, poultry and salads. See also Chart (pages 140–141).

FIVE-SPICE POWDER

This is the mixture of spices used in authentic Chinese cookery.

15 g ($\frac{1}{2}$ oz) anise pepper
15 g ($\frac{1}{2}$ oz) star anise
15 g ($\frac{1}{2}$ oz) cassia bark or cinnamon stick
15 g ($\frac{1}{2}$ oz) whole cloves
15 g ($\frac{1}{2}$ oz) fennel seed

Grind together all the spices. Store in an airtight jar. Keeps for up to one month.

PICKLING SPICE

This is a basic mixture for pickles and chutneys. Different spices can be added according to taste and availability. For example, some contain whole chillies, giving a hotter flavour. Coriander seeds, juniper berries and mustard seeds can also be added.

30 ml (2 tbsp) mace blades
15 ml (1 tbsp) allspice berries
15 ml (1 tbsp) whole cloves
18-cm (7-inch) cinnamon stick
6 black peppercorns
1 bay leaf, crumbled

Mix all the ingredients together well. Store in an airtight, screw-topped jar. Keeps well for up to 1 month. Tie in a muslin bag to use.

GARAM MASALA

This is a basic recipe for the mixture of ground spices which is frequently used in Indian cookery; the amounts can be increased or decreased according to taste and spices such as dried red chillies or whole coriander may be added.

4 black cardamoms or 10 green cardamoms
15 ml (1 tbsp) black peppercorns
10 ml (2 tsp) cumin seeds

MIXED SPICE

15 g ($\frac{1}{2}$ oz) whole cloves
15 g ($\frac{1}{2}$ oz) ground ginger
15 g ($\frac{1}{2}$ oz) whole allspice berries
12.5 cm (5 inch) stick cinnamon
1.25 ml ($\frac{1}{4}$ tsp) black peppercorns
25 g (1 oz) freshly grated nutmeg

Grind the whole spices together and mix with the nutmeg and ginger. Store in an airtight, screw-topped jar. Keeps well for up to 1 month. Use for baking and in puddings.

CURRY POWDER

30 ml (2 tbsp) cumin seeds
30 ml (2 tbsp) whole fenugreek
7.5 ml (1$\frac{1}{4}$ tsp) mustard seed
15 ml (1 tbsp) black peppercorns
120 ml (8 tbsp) coriander seeds
15 ml (1 tbsp) poppy seeds
15 ml (1 tbsp) ground ginger
5 ml (1 tsp) chilli powder
60 ml (4 tbsp) ground turmeric

Combine all the ingredients in an electric blender or coffee grinder and blend to a fine powder. Store in an airtight container. Will keep for up to 3 months.

COCONUT MILK

**flesh from one large fresh
    coconut**
100 ml (4 fl oz) hot water

1 Grate the coconut flesh. Add
the water and leave to soak for
20 minutes.

2 With clean hands, pick up the
grated coconut and squeeze it
into the bowl to extract all the
liquid.

3 If a larger amount of thinner
milk is required, add a further
150 ml ($\frac{1}{4}$ pint) water to the
squeezed coconut. Leave it for 20
minutes and squeeze again. Discard the coconut.

——— VARIATION ———

To make coconut milk with coconut cream, dissolve **50 g (2 oz)
creamed coconut in 150 ml ($\frac{1}{4}$
pint) warm water**. This will
make a thick milk. For a thinner
one, add extra water.

TAMARIND JUICE

15 ml (1 tbsp) dried tamarind pulp
60 ml (4 tbsp) warm water

1 Soak the dried pulp in warm
water for 15 minutes. Strain
the liquid through a sieve, pressing down hard with a wooden
spoon to extract as much of the
pulp as possible.

2 Discard the pulp left in the
sieve and use the juice according to the recipe.

DRINKS
GLÜHWEIN

Makes about 700 ml (1$\frac{1}{4}$ pints)

600 ml (1 pint) red wine
75 g (3 oz) dark soft brown sugar
**two 12.5-cm (5-inch) sticks
    cinnamon**
1 lemon, stuck with 10 whole cloves
150 ml ($\frac{1}{4}$ pint) brandy

Put all ingredients except brandy
into a pan. Bring to simmering
point; simmer gently, covered, for
2–4 minutes. Remove from heat.
Add brandy. Strain into warmed
bowl and serve.

CHRISTMAS WINE

Makes about 2.4 litres (4$\frac{1}{4}$ pints)

1 bottle aquavit or gin
2 bottles burgundy
75 g (3 oz) raisins
100 g (4 oz) sugar
6 cloves
5-cm (2-inch) cinnamon stick
thinly pared strip of lemon rind

1 Put half the aquavit into a
saucepan with the burgundy.
Add raisins and sugar. Tie spices
and lemon rind in muslin and put
into pan. Cover. Bring slowly to
boil and simmer for 30 minutes.
Add remaining aquavit and remove from heat.

2 Strain into a bowl. Before
serving, ignite drink. Ladle
into tumblers.

MULLED ALE
(Modern version)

Makes about 1 litre (2 pints)

1 lemon
600 ml (1 pint) brown ale
60 ml (4 tbsp) brandy
30 ml (2 tbsp) rum
30 ml (2 tbsp) gin
30 ml (2 tbsp) demerara sugar
300 ml ($\frac{1}{2}$ pint) water
1.25 ml ($\frac{1}{4}$ tsp) grated nutmeg
1.25 ml ($\frac{1}{4}$ tsp) ground cinnamon

Pare the lemon thinly and squeeze
out the juice. Put the rind and
juice with all the other ingredients
into a large pan and heat to just
below boiling point. Strain and
serve at once in punch glasses.

18th CENTURY
MULLED ALE

Makes about 1.7 litres (3 pints)

1.2 litres (2 pints) brown ale
grated rind of $\frac{1}{2}$ lemon
5 ml (1 tsp) ground ginger
5 ml (1 tsp) grated nutmeg
75 g (3 oz) dark soft brown sugar
3 eggs
150 ml (5 fl oz) brandy
150 ml (5 fl oz) rum

1 Heat the ale with the lemon
rind and spices to boiling
point. Meanwhile, make a clean
poker red hot. Plunge it into the
ale and hold it there until the
seething subsides.

2 Whip the sugar and eggs together until frothy. Warm the
brandy and rum together in a
small pan. Pour them into the ale.
Pour in the eggs. Pour the whole
back and forth from one pan to
another until smooth and creamy.
Serve at once.

MULLED CLARET

Makes about 1.4 litres (2½ pints)

1 litre (1¾ pints) claret

thinly pared rind of 1 orange

thinly pared rind of 1 lemon

12–16 sugar lumps

5 ml (1 tsp) mixed ground
cinnamon and grated nutmeg

2 bay leaves

300 ml (½ pint) brandy

Heat the claret with the orange and lemon rind, sugar, spices and bay leaves. Heat the brandy in a separate pan but do not boil. Take claret and brandy to place of serving. Pour wine into a warmed, heat-resistant bowl. Add hot brandy and ignite. Ladle into glasses while still flaming.

MULLED WINE

Makes about 900 ml (1½ pints)

300 ml (½ pint) water

100 g (4 oz) sugar

4 cloves

5-cm (2-inch) stick cinnamon

2 lemons, thinly sliced

1 bottle burgundy or claret

1 orange, thinly sliced, to decorate

Heat first 4 ingredients until sugar has dissolved, then bring to the boil. Add the lemon slices, stir and leave to stand for 10 minutes. Pour in wine. Heat but do not boil. Strain into a serving bowl and serve hot, decorated with orange slices.

VIRGINIA MINT JULEP

Serves 1

9 fresh mint leaves

5 ml (1 tsp) sugar or sugar syrup

crushed ice

1 measure Bourbon whisky

Put 6 mint leaves into a cold glass. Add the sugar and crush it with the leaves. Fill the glass with crushed ice. Pour in the whisky, stirring well. Serve immediately decorated with remaining leaves.

SPICY FRUIT PUNCH

Makes about 2.8 litres (5 pints)

600 ml (1 pint) natural orange juice

300 ml (½ pint) pineapple juice

thinly pared rind and juice of 1
lemon

2.5 ml (½ tsp) grated nutmeg

6 cloves

2.5 ml (½ tsp) ground mixed spice

600 ml (1 pint) water

100 g (4 oz) sugar

6 splits ginger ale, chilled

crushed ice

twists of lemon or orange peel, to
decorate

Mix the fruit juices, lemon rind and spices in a large jug. Put the water and sugar into a saucepan and heat gently to dissolve the sugar. Cool. Add the syrup to the other ingredients in the jug. Chill. Strain and add the ginger ale and some crushed ice before serving. Decorate with the peel.

———— VARIATION ————

Try using natural apple juice or grapefruit juice instead of orange and pineapple juice and add ground cinnamon instead of grated nutmeg. Decorate with thin slices of orange or lemon and a sprig of fresh mint, if you wish.

HERB TEAS

Herbal teas, or tisanes, have for a long time been popular in Europe, but it has not been until recently that they have been rediscovered in Britain.

You can now readily buy packets of single herbs and herb mixtures for making into teas, and many are also available in tea bag form.

If you drink tisanes, a wide variety of healthy hot drinks is available to you as each one has its own flavour and qualities. Some are reviving and refreshing, others calming and soothing. Some have a sweet, honeyed flavour and others are sharp or slightly bitter.

Herbal teas can be made with fresh or dried herbs. Make them in a tea pot with boiling water in exactly the same way as you would ordinary tea.

Per cup, you will need 15 ml (1 tbsp) chopped fresh herbs or 5 ml (1 tsp) dried.

Herbs which make good tisanes include angelica, balm, bergamot, caraway, chamomile, comfrey, fennel, hibiscus, lime flowers, lemon verbena, marjoram, peppermint, spearmint and sage.

RELAXING TISANE

25 g (1 oz) dried lime flowers

25 g (1 oz) dried lemon balm

7 g (¼ oz) dried marjoram

Make as directed above.

REFRESHING TISANE

25 g (1 oz) dried rosehips

15 g (½ oz) dried peppermint

15 g (½ oz) dried hibiscus

5 ml (1 tsp) dried grated lemon peel

Make as directed above.

INDEX